BADMINTON

Barry C. Pelton

BADMINTON

Prentice-Hall, Inc., Englewood Cliffs, New Jersey

CONTENTS

I
The
First
Step

APPENDIX
badminton rules   61

GLOSSARY OF TERMS   69

SELECTED REFERENCES AND READINGS   75

INDEX   83

FOREWORD

I feel greatly honored and pleased to have the opportunity of congratulating the author for his contribution to the sport of badminton. In the United States today there are two facets of badminton: the game and the sport. Millions of Americans are acquainted with the game of badminton, unfortunately very few have ever seen or even considered badminton as a competitive sport.

Having started playing badminton in the backyard myself, I was utterly amazed at the great skill strategy, speed, endurance, and competitiveness required when I first saw tournament badminton. However, only through playing can one really appreciate the deceptiveness, teamwork, and strategy involved in competitive badminton. Besides being able to compete at local, regional, national, and international levels, badminton offers many other attractions for its participants. It is a relatively inexpensive sport, offers competition for and between both sexes, and is played both competitively and for recreation by people between the ages of 8 and 60+ years. The entire family can participate both socially and competitively, not to mention the obvious values gained through the development of sportsmanship and physical fitness. Most important to me, however, has been the years of enjoyment gained from playing badminton regardless of the caliber of play. I have yet to meet anyone who has not found playing badminton to be fun.

Should one be fortunate enough to achieve success at a national level, badminton offers many opportunities for one to compete and represent his country all over the world, as well as hosting foreign players in America. To give some idea of the scope of badminton in foreign lands, I have seen children carrying badminton rackets to school in Malaysia and Thailand; the Indonesian Congress stood for 15 minutes in tribute to Rudy Hartono for winning the All-England Badminton Championships (symbolizing world champion) in hopes his accomplishment would help them strive to have a better legislative session; and Erland Kops is known to every Danish child as is Babe Ruth in America. In Europe and Asia thousands of spectators crowd to the major tournaments, whereas in the United States hardly this many people really know the existence of tournament badminton.

With all the benefits derived from playing badminton, two crucial obstacles need to be overcome before the sport rises in popularity as it has in many foreign countries. First is the problem of acquainting people with the sport, and second is the teaching of basic badminton skills.

This text is designed to solve these obstacles through widespread distribution and the author's compilation of a consensus of the successful techniques from other published sources and adopting them for teaching badminton skills. It is anticipated this publication authored by an experienced physical education instructor and badminton player will contribute materially in bridging the gap between badminton as a game and badminton as a life-time sport.

Donald C. Paup
U. S. National Open
Mens Doubles Badminton

PREFACE

The purpose of this text is to provide individuals with a complete reference for learning to play the game of badminton. This text is geared toward self-instruction, a feature that should appeal to beginners, but it should also be of value to the individual who wishes to pursue badminton skills to a more advanced level.

Personal judgment as to the selection of skills to be learned, technique and procedures for learning these skills, and methods of evaluating achievement has been exercised. However, the text is as scientifically oriented as possible with the hope of validating claims that badminton is a game of recreational carryover value and one that may enhance total fitness, which leads to the fully enriched life.

Specifically, chapters identifying the physiological, psychological and motor characteristics considered essential to playing the game are presented. Necessary equipment, facilities, rules, and sportsmanship are discussed. Stroking techniques are illustrated by means of strobe photographs. Line drawings that illustrate court placement areas, flight patterns, and court positions are presented.

Fundamentals of sound strategy and safety principles are included, along with the historical development and philosophic bases of the game. An additional special feature of this text is that an attempt is made to substantiate, through documentation and research, traditional claims as to the actual values and benefits from participation in the game. The basic mechanical principles of movement involved are explained and analyzed, and the learning principles that apply to the game are identified. The book proposes a program of physical conditioning and training, and provides a complete glossary of badminton terms and a suggested bibliography of additional references.

Even though this text is primarily designed for college-age youth, it should be of value to any young person or adult who aspires to learn to play the game of badminton.

B.C.P.

1

BADMINTON AND THE INDIVIDUAL

You now need to:
1. Have a clear concept of physical fitness
2. Know the physical qualities, psychological qualities, and motor capacity considered essential to the badminton player
3. Realize contraindications to playing in the game of badminton

In general, this book is intended for the beginning badminton player, but guidelines are included for those who wish to work toward the advanced level of play.

Participation in any sports activity requires certain basic individual qualities. Badminton is no exception. Age level will largely determine the physiological and psychological qualities, and degree of motor capacity the participant displays.

1. The age of the participant may range from that of upper elementary school to over 65.

2. Specific physiological qualifications, psychological qualifications, and motor capacities influence successful play.

3. Additional understanding, skills, and strategies are required for championship play.

PHYSICAL FITNESS

Before you can attain optimum physical fitness, you must ask yourself several questions and identify the various physiological qualities that constitute fitness, particularly those relevant to badminton. A first question is: What is physical fitness? "Freedom from disease" and "freedom from a pathological condition or physical disability" are definitions often given but they are *not* widely accepted among physical educators. (Hunsicker)

For our purpose, fitness may be defined as "that state which characterizes the degree to which the person is able to function." (Morgan, 1960). Fitness is a dynamic and changing quality. The American Association for Health, Physical Education, and Recreation includes the following as constituents of fitness.

1. Optimum organic health consistent with heredity and the application of present health knowledge.

2. Sufficient coordination, strength, and vitality to meet emergencies, as well as the requirements of daily living.

3. Emotional stability to meet the stresses and strains of modern life.

4. Social consciousness and adaptability with respect to the requirements of group living.

5. Sufficient knowledge and insight to make suitable decisions and arrive at feasible solutions to problems.

6. Attitudes, values, and skills which stimulate satisfactory participation in a full range of daily activities.

7. Spiritual and moral qualities which contribute to the fullest measure of living in a democratic society (Karpovich, 1953).

The term *physical fitness* is used to describe fitness of the body or as one authority puts it, "the adaptability or suitability to some particular muscle stress" (Cratty, 1964). Strictly speaking, physical fitness is considered one element of the total person and his competence to risk a task involving muscular action.

QUALITIES OF A BADMINTON PLAYER

Physical Qualities

With respect to performance of a motor skill such as badminton, simply stated, the physically fit individuals will likely be more psychologically stable than the individuals who are at a lower level of fitness, when both are given the same task. In addition, the fit performer should recover more quickly after the task has been performed.

The following common aspects of physical fitness and motor ability are most important to the badminton performer: strength of certain muscle groups, muscular endurance, agility, cardiorespiratory efficiency, speed, balance, and neuromuscular coordination.

The interrelationships of the aforementioned are not known to be high. However, the more of these physiological qualities you possess, the closer you will be to total fitness. The following general statements are of importance to you as you work toward the level of fitness required to play badminton at your best.

1. Your physical fitness status can be improved upon if you are willing to exert the energy.

2. Physical fitness requires vigorous activity and a high expenditure of energy.

3. High-level physical fitness is not a permanent state. Once you have attained your desired level of fitness you must work to maintain it.

4. Physical fitness is interrelated with mental fitness. You must give fitness a high-level priority in your value system.

5. Physical fitness is a lifelong involvement. Research concludes that decline in body contour and physical performance are reduced by the consistent maintenance of a high level of physical fitness.

6. Physical fitness results in weight control, which is part of good personal appearance. The male can build and improve his musculature through a good program of physical fitness. At the same time the female need not fear of becoming overly muscular from a vigorous fitness program. A suggested program will be presented in Chapter 6.

Badminton has been found to be a game that contributes to physical fitness, especially cardiovascular capacity and endurance and flexibility (Hunsicker). Further, individuals who exercise regularly claim that they have "a general feeling of well-being." Hence, it is logical and possible that "complex biochemical and neurophysiological changes take place and cause the sensation of feeling better" (Cratty, 1968). The important factor is to determine your attainable level of fitness based upon your age and physiological capacities and status.

Psychological Qualities

Broadly defined, the psychological aspect of sports participation refers to the mental nature of performance. Some research suggests that individuals with certain personality traits select or tend to choose certain sports, but evidence is not sufficient. Nor is there sufficient evidence to support the claim that certain sports actually modify the personality traits of the individual. However, according to Cratty (1964), an individual cannot perform at a level beyond that permitted by the response capacities of his nervous system. Effective locomotion, or performance in this case, is integrated with mental response. Cratty suggests three factors that influence perceptual-motor behavior. The first factor is *skill specifics* that involve practice and practice conditions in a task. The second factor is *physical ability traits,* including strength, movement speed, and gross agility. The third factor is *basic behaviorial supports*, including ability to: (1) analyze the task, (2) manipulate tension level, (3) persist when subjected to discomfort, (4) feel a need for achievement and mastery, and (5) experience a need for social approval.

The following general statements identify specifically the psychological qualities involved in playing badminton successfully.

1. You must be patient, inasmuch as improvement in the acquisition of skill in games requiring refined movements is slower than in those games involving gross motor movements.

2. You must understand the task and be able to apply constructive self-criticism, and accept constructive criticism.

3. You must persevere in your desire to learn and include learning to play badminton as a part of your set of values.

4. You must be able to work successfully in groups and individually as you seek to improve.

5. You must understand the involvements of competition and maintain a wholesome viewpoint toward winning and losing.

6. You must maintain a high level of aspiration and motivation in order to improve.

Research evidence that supports the relationship between perceptual components and motor performance is increasing. Failure to accept the existence of this relationship no doubt affects the learning of motor skills. Regardless of the age level of the participant or the level of competition, each playing situation is heavily charged with emotions, each of which influences in some manner the performance of the skill.

Motor Capacity

Cratty (1964) proposes that a precise understanding of the term *motor capacity* can best be gained by considering related terms. *Movement behavior* refers to observable movements of the skeletal muscle, i.e., the gross movement of the body. Movement behavior is considered to be synonymous with *motor behavior. Motor performance* is, for our purposes, the planned, purposeful act of playing badminton. *Motor skill* refers to the performance of a motor task, in our case badminton. *Motor learning* refers to a change, usually permanent, in motor behavior (such as in playing badminton). *Motor capacity*, for our purpose, refers to the capacity to learn a motor skill.

Individuals vary in their capacity to learn a motor skill. Among the factors that directly affect one's motor capacity are coordination, agility, strength, eye-hand coordination, balance, speed, and neuromuscular skill. Most individuals can learn to contact the shuttlecock and rally back and forth across the net. However, the ability to maneuver on the court, anticipate the opponent's actions, or improve on finesse and power shots is contingent upon basic motor capacity. Therefore, it is important for you to determine as accurately as possible your level of potential to perform refined motor tasks, so that you may set your ultimate goal of performance and avoid frustration when skill improvement is slow.

CONTRAINDICATIONS: WHO SHOULD NOT PLAY BADMINTON?

The term *contraindications* implies that negative results are possible as well as positive results from playing badminton if the individual does not have certain physical and mental characteristics.

Physical Qualities

Men with angular physiques resembling the track man's musculature are usually more suited than others to the requirements of badminton. Height may vary from very short (as in most Malaysian, Indonesian, and Asiatic players) to the average height of the U. S. male. Explosive muscle power is an asset, particularly among men, but is often overshadowed by exceptional reaction time, endurance, recovery of balance, and overall qualities of movement within a small court area.

Mental Qualities

Individuals with a skill in quick analysis of play situations are usually more successful in badminton, other qualities of the players being equal. The ability to detect an opponent's strengths and weaknesses, and general patterns of strategy are assets to the individual.

An individual who does not permit lasting emotional outbursts following a good shot by his opponent, a questionable decision by an official, or audience reaction is in an advantageous position.

Playing badminton offers an opportunity for cooperation and competition. Men usually emphasize competition, whereas women more often emphasize cooperation. Players who can rationally adjust to these contrasting situations are generally in a better mental frame of mind than others to participate satisfactorily.

The interrelationships of physiological, psychological, and motor capacity for badminton are complex. Participation in badminton will not change you into an entirely different person. If you have entered into this sport voluntarily, if the playing experience is vigorous and wholesome, if the instruction is good, and if the measurement of achievement is logical, then you should attain skilled performance and you will thoroughly enjoy the game.

INDIVIDUAL DIFFERENCES IN PHYSIOLOGICAL AND PSYCHOLOGICAL MAKEUP AND MOTOR PERFORMANCE POTENTIAL MAY:

Influence the learning rate noticeably.
Determine level of skill attainment.
Affect form in stroke production.

2

THE CHALLENGE
playing the game

This chapter will acquaint you with:
1. Badminton facilities and equipment
2. Rules of the game
3. Cautions and safety principles
4. Sportsmanship principles

Games require proper facilities and equipment before they can be enjoyed to the fullest extent. Badminton is a game that fortunately may be played in a variety of settings requiring very little special equipment.

FACILITIES AND EQUIPMENT

Badminton may be played either indoors or outdoors. The dimensions for the court are shown in Figure 2-1. If the game is played outdoors, the surface may be cement, asphalt, hard packed dirt, clay, or short cropped grass like that used in lawn tennis. You can even play in your own backyard.

Indoor courts are usually more enjoyable because the wind does not interfere and you can play throughout the year. Most official tournaments and championships are played indoors. Occasionally, special exhibitions are played outdoors.

Equipment for the game of badminton depends upon the setting. If you are playing at home or at a recreation center you can select a variety of types of rubber soled athletic shoes, shorts,

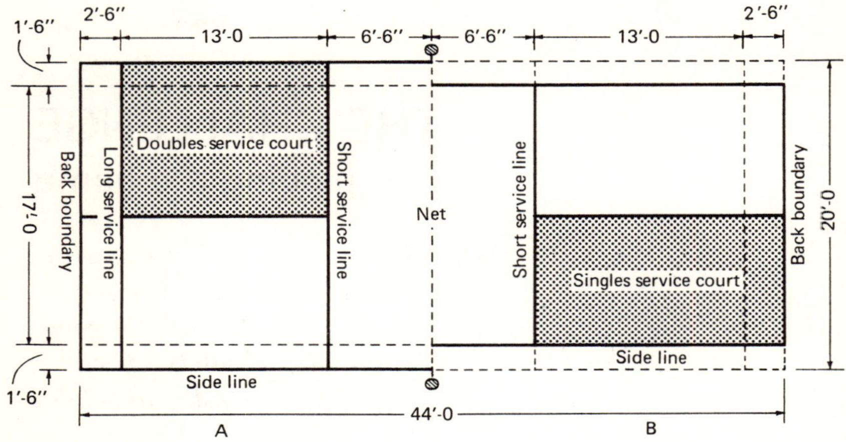

FIGURE 2-1. Court dimensions

shirts, and inexpensive to very expensive rackets. If you are playing in a tournament, you may choose all-white apparel, white shoes, and a more expensive racket.

You should get assistance from a qualified person when selecting your racket and playing apparel. The shuttlecock may be cork-tipped and made with feathers, the type usually preferred as the level of skill improves; or plastic, sometimes preferred for outdoor play because the flight pattern is less affected by the wind.

The racket resembles a tennis racket and is usually made of aluminum, fiberglass, wood, or plastic. It may be strung with nylon, gut, or linen strings. Because of its light weight and delicate appearance, you may think that it is not durable. However, if care is taken to keep the racket in a dry place when not in use and in a frame or press, which prevents warping, it should last indefinitely. To protect the racket, do not strike the court with it or lean your weight on it between points.

The shuttlecock is a fascinating aspect of the game. One type has a base of cork with 16 feathers arranged around the edge. The feathers should be straightened between points.

This type of shuttlecock weighs only one-sixth of an ounce and is more expensive than the plastic type. The plastic shuttlecock is constructed in the same manner as the feathered one but without feathers and with a rubber tip.

Participants

It is essential that attention be given to the choice or pairing of participants if the game is to be enjoyed to its fullest extent. Players with commensurate playing abilities should oppose each other on a regular basis to assure proper motivation and opportunities for self-actualization. Mismatches require a tremendous amount of understanding and self-sacrifice, which are possible only among true friends and in effective student-teacher relationships. It is pointed out as a unique feature of badminton that women and men may compete satisfactorily even though men usually evidence a more explosive repertoire of strokes; their power may be offset by women's movement patterns.

Sportsmanship Principles

The ancient Greek concept of competition is very applicable to contemporary theories of sportsmanship. The Greeks believed that one should compete with his opponent to produce the highest individual excellence in performance of which he was capable. Essential traits of good sportsmanship are few. Following these principles should guarantee enjoyable participation, regardless of the outcome of the game.

1. Quality equipment should be used, and when playing where shuttlecocks are not provided, you should provide your share of the shuttlecocks.

2. If there is no official referee, call shots quickly, because reflexes and movements of your opponent are contingent upon your decision. Always give your opponent the benefit of the doubt on close decisions.

3. Call the official score after each point or rally.

4. Avoid loud verbal outbursts or racket throwing.

5. During warmups, keep the shuttlecock in play, giving your opponent an opportunity to practice all shots.

6. At the conclusion of a practice session or a match, be sincere and shake hands, regardless of the outcome.

7. In mixed doubles, apply all courtesies to the lady—a habit that befits both informal or formal playing situations.

Even though the Olympic motto was written specifically for Olympic competition, it seems applicable to any sports activity: "It's not who won or lost, but how you played the game."

THE RULES OF BADMINTON

In order to play badminton one must possess a working knowledge of the rules governing the sport. This section represents an interpretation of the official rules, which appear in the appendix. Game situations are presented as a simplified version or popularization of the precise rules.

Singles Play

The opponents will first "toss" or spin a racket to determine which player will serve first or be allowed to select an end of the court. The side losing the toss will get to select the remaining alternative.

Play will start from the right service court with the serve. When serving the players must be in their respective courts and in a stationary position. When delivering the serve, the player must contact the shuttle below the waist and the racket may not be higher than the server's hand. The shuttle must fall into the court diagonally opposite the server.

The receiver will return the shuttle and play will continue until one player fails to make a return or commits a fault. It is a fault if the shuttle falls outside the boundaries of the court, fails to go over the net, or goes through the net. A player is also guilty of a fault if he strikes the shuttlecock before it crosses the net, touches the net with his racket or body, or commits a "carry." In such cases a player either wins a point or loses his term of service. Points are scored only by the server.

If the server wins the point he continues serving; the second serve is delivered from the left-hand service court. His term of service lasts until he is guilty of a fault or fails to hit the serve into the proper court. At this time the second player serves his first service from the right service court. He continues serving, alternating courts, until he loses his serve. After the initial serve for each player in a game, the score will determine the service court. If a player's score is 1, 3, or any other *odd* number he will deliver the serve from the *left* court. If the score is 0, 2, or any other *even* number the serve will be made from the right service court. Play continues until one player reaches 11 points (in a ladies' singles game) or 15 or 21 points (in a men's game).

A player does not have to win by two points. However, under certain circumstances a player has the option of "setting" a game. This occurs when the score is 9-all or 10-all in the ladies' singles game, 13-all or 14-all in the ladies' doubles or men's game, or 19-all or 20-all in a game of 21 points. If the score is 9-all the game may be set to 3; 10-all, set to 2; 13-all or 19-all, set to

5; and 14-all or 20-all, to 3. In such cases the score becomes "love-all" and play continues until one player reaches the designated number of points. The first player reaching the score of 9-all, 13-all, and so forth has the option of setting the game. If he refuses, a game can be set only if the score is once again tied at 10-all, 14-all, and so forth. Once again the first player reaching the score first has the option of setting.

Although the score becomes love-all in a game that has been set, the serving order continues in the prescribed manner, e.g., the next service after a 9-all game has been set will be delivered from the left court, even though the score is called love-all, because 9 is an odd number. If a game is set at 10-all, the next service will be from the right court because 10 is an even number.

Doubles Play

The same rules concerning singles play apply to the doubles game, the exceptions being the order of serving and receiving. The game begins by tossing or spinning the racket, the winner having the options of serving or end of court. The following differences are noted.

1. The team that serves first has only one term of service or "in-side"; thereafter, both members of the team will serve.

2. The first serve is always delivered from the right court. (See Fig. 2-2 for service courts.)

3. Only the player served to may return the service.

4. The serving order for each team must be maintained and is determined by the score.

To illustrate the fourth point: at the beginning of a game team player A serves. Player A scores a point and delivers the second serve from the left service court. Player A's team loses this point and the term of service ends, as explained in number 1 above. Both members of team B will now have a term of service. The first server, B 1, loses his serve but the second server, B 2, scores three points before his team commits a fault. The service then reverts to the other team and *both* players on team A will now have a term of service. The first serve will be delivered from the right court and A 2 will serve first. This is because the score is 1-3 (calling the serving team's score first), which places A 1 in the left court. When team B regains the serve, B 2 serves first. In other words, if the team's score is even, the players serve and receive in the court in which they originally began serving. If the score is odd, the team members will be serving or receiving in the court in which they did not start, or their odd courts.

Additional rules for both singles and doubles are these. During the serve, if the server swings and misses the shuttlecock it is not a fault. If the shuttlecock touches the net in flight to the opponent's service court it is considered in play, not a "let" as in tennis.

CAUTIONS AND SAFETY PRINCIPLES

Active participation in a vigorous activity involves specific responsibilities on the part of the participant and the teacher. Careful attention to these factors should provide a healthful and safe playing experience.

1. If possible, a selected conditioning program should precede or at least accompany participation.

2. A physical examination should be given each participant if the participant has a medical history that would indicate possible harm from participation.

3. Proper equipment and facilities are important aspects of safety. Equipment and facilities should be provided and maintained properly.

It should be stressed that badminton is more enjoyable if the rules are strictly followed and the unwritten rules of good sportsmanship are exemplified. For example, make certain that your opponent is ready before serving. Call the server's score first and before each point. Be considerate of play on adjacent courts. Call all shots quickly and fairly. If the point is contestable give your opponent the benefit of the doubt or replay the point.

You should not minimize the safety suggestions involved in any sport. They are an integral part of the game. Overlooking them leads to inferior performance, decrease in enjoyment, and undesirable physical and psychological reactions.

YOU SHOULD ALWAYS KEEP IN MIND THAT:

Proper equipment and facilities are essential when playing badminton if one is to enjoy the game to the fullest.

Play is usually more enjoyable and improvement in skill is more readily attained if opponents are of commensurate ability.

General safety precautions are appropriate in all sports. Ignoring them may lead to inferior performance, decrease in enjoyment, and undesirable physical and psychological reactions.

Good sportsmanship always increases the enjoyment of human interaction in sport.

3

BASIC SKILLS

This chapter explains how to:
1. Assume the proper grip for forehand
*   and backhand strokes*
2. Assume the proper playing or ready position
3. Employ correct footwork for each stroke
4. Execute fundamental strokes
5. Apply basic techniques and strategy to actual
*   playing situations in singles and doubles*

The skills described in this chapter are those all beginning players will need to master before attempting to learn the more advanced skills. All instruction is geared to right-handed players and must be reversed for the left-handed player.

GRIPS

The most popular grips in badminton are similar to those grips popular in tennis. (See Fig. 3-1.) Either the forehand or the backhand grip is generally used for all strokes in badminton. The forehand grip is achieved by holding the racket in the left hand at the throat with the face of the racket perpendicular to the playing surface. Simply shake hands with the racket. Place the hand as near the end of the area where the racket is gripped as you can to assure optimum wrist action. Grip the racket firmly with fingers closed around the handle for power shots and more loosely for finesse shots. To achieve the backhand grip, turn the hand counterclockwise until the *V* formed by your thumb and forefinger is on top of the area where the racket is gripped. You may now

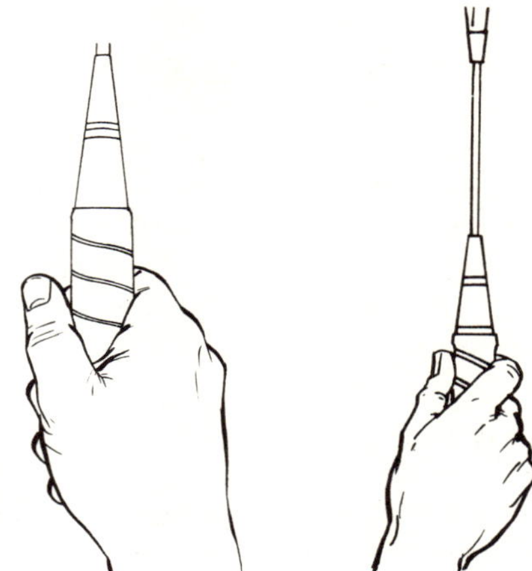

FIGURE 3-1. Grip. (A) Forehand; (B) backhand. Note that the thumb closes around the grip in the forehand; in the backhand it is extended down the back of the grip.

leave the thumb flat and extended against the back of the racket or encircle the racket as in the forehand.

PLAYING POSITION

The playing position or ready position is very important. The precise area of the court is in relation to the playing situation, i.e., whether you are playing

FIGURE 3-2. Playing position, front view. The arrow indicates the range in which players may choose to position the racket while waiting to receive. The left arm may also be raised.

singles or doubles, whether you are serving or receiving, or the area into which your opponent has maneuvered you. The weight should be distributed evenly on the balls of your feet. The feet are spread approximately to shoulder width or whatever distance you find comfortable, necessary in acquiring good body balance, and necessary for quick movements. The knees should be slightly bent. The racket should be held in front of the body with the wrist and grip at approximately waist level, and the head of the racket higher (see Fig. 3-2). Precise positioning of the body and racket may vary among individuals, but a good alert ready position is essential to good play.

FOOTWORK

Correct footwork is important for those players who wish to improve their skill. Hints for good footwork:

1. Assume the ready position.

2. When attempting to hit any shot to the right side of the body, pivot or turn on the balls of the feet, take the necessary steps to reach the shuttlecock with the right foot leading, and make certain your left side is slightly toward the net when you stroke.

3. When attempting to hit any shot to the left side of the body, pivot or turn the balls of the feet and step or lead with the left foot. Your right shoulder should be toward the net when you stroke.

4. A bouncing or sliding motion is a very effective means of making quick movements in badminton. Never stand flat-footed while waiting for a shot or when moving toward the shuttlecock.

FUNDAMENTAL STROKES

The following skills are considered to be essential for you to master and should provide you with a sufficient repertoire of strokes to enable you to enjoy a good all-round game. Skills needed by advanced players will be presented in a later chapter. The order in which you learn the fundamental skills will no doubt vary, depending upon the amount of formal instruction. Many experts in the game suggest the following order.

Service

The serve is an underhand stroke and may be hit with either a forehand or a backhand grip. The forehand grip is most commonly used. The head of the

FIGURE 3-3. The service

racket must be below the level of your hand, and the shuttlecock must be contacted below the level of your waist.

The court area from which you serve is important. The following hints are helpful in learning to serve. (See Fig. 3-3.)

1. Stand several inches from the center line of the service area and about two to three feet from the short service line.

2. The left foot should be slightly forward, and both knees slightly flexed. Remember, both feet must remain in contact with the court surface.

3. Assume the forehand grip.

4. Hold the shuttle by the tip of several feathers or at the base of the shuttlecock with the thumb and forefinger of the left hand.

5. Extend the left arm diagonally across the body at about shoulder level.

6. The racket is taken back at waist level or higher.

7. As the racket is brought forward in a downward sweeping motion, drop the shuttlecock. The point of contact is between knee and waist level. During the entire process of the serve, the weight of the body is shifted from the left foot to the right foot and back to the left foot.

8. The follow-through is important. Inasmuch as the serve is an underhand stroke, the follow-through will be upward in the direction of the desired placement area. Too short a follow-through will result in the shuttlecock's going into an undesired direction.

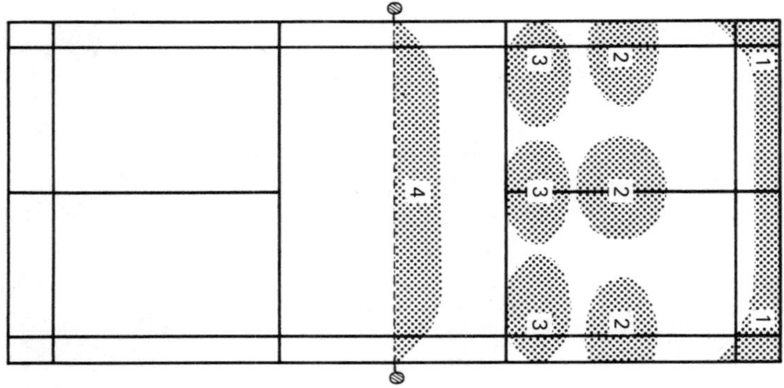

FIGURE 3-4. Placement areas. (1) Clears and high serves; (2) smashes and drives; (3) Half-smashes, push-shots, and low serves; (4) dropshots and hairpin net shots.

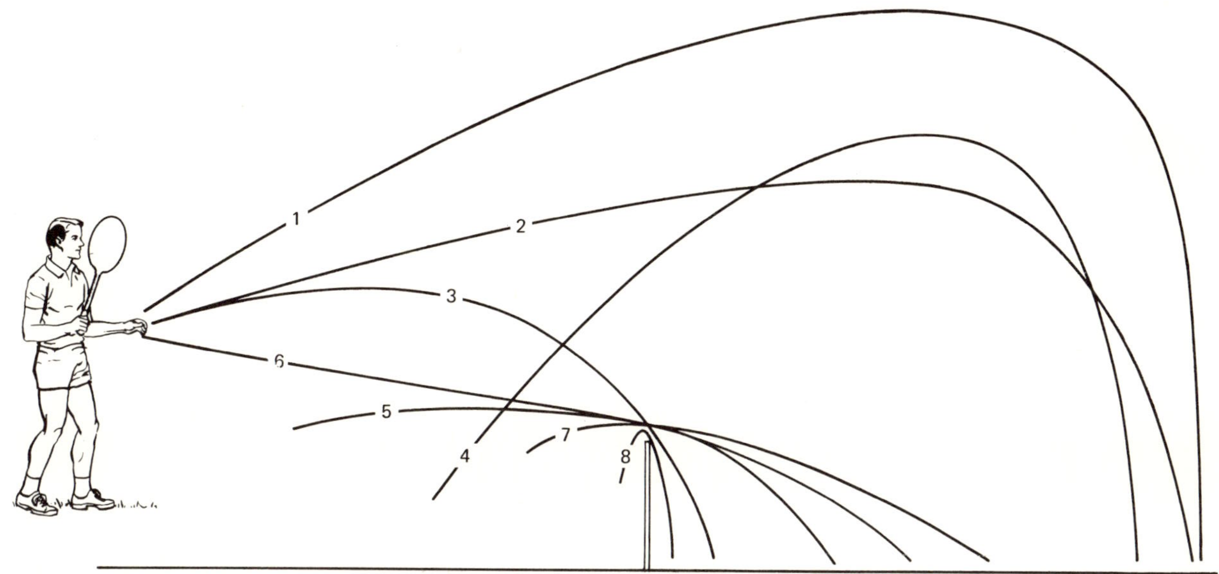

FIGURE 3-5. Basic flight patterns. (1) Defensive clear; (2) attacking clear; (3) overhead dropshot; (4) high dropshot; (5) midcourt drive; (6) half smash; (7) push shot; (8) Hairpin netshot.

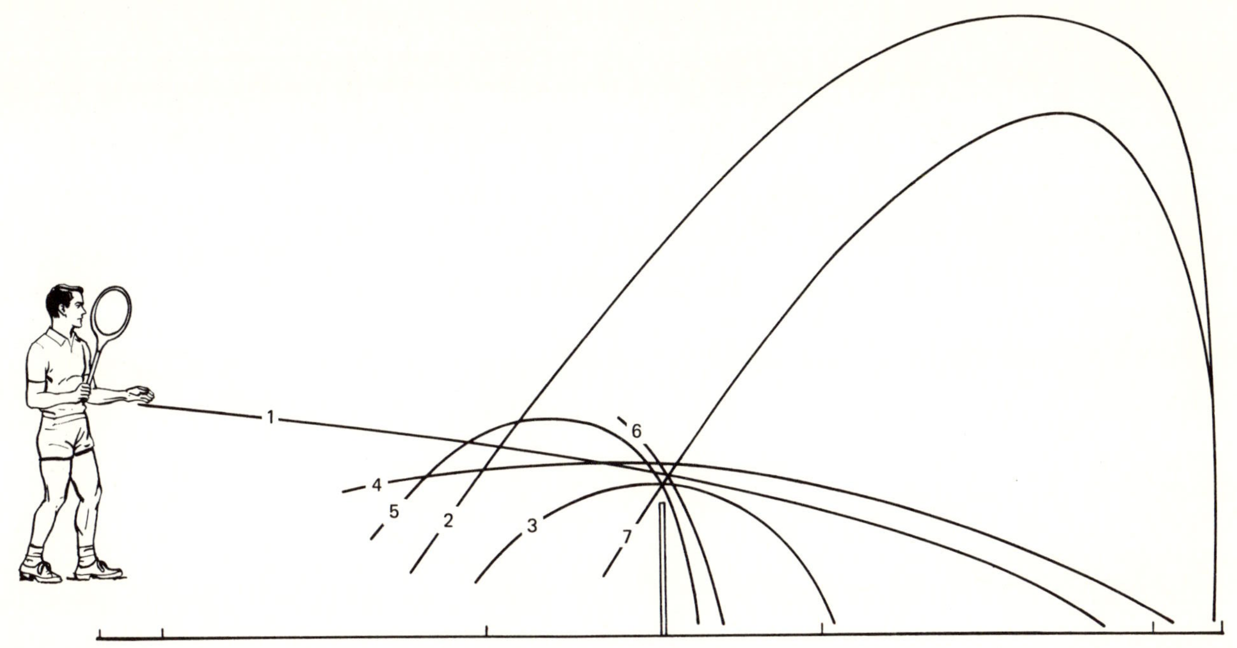

FIGURE 3-6. Additional flight patterns. (1) Smash; (2) high singles serve; (3) low doubles serve; (4) drive; (5) underhand dropshot; (6) net smash; (7) underhand clear.

Types of Service

Look at Fig. 3-3 for service stroking techniques. Look at Fig 3-4 for placement areas. The short service or low service is the one used most often in doubles. This service requires little power or force and is almost guided over the net.

The forehand grip is usually used for hitting this service. The type of service forces the receiver to return with a short low return or a high shot, which may be smashed or killed. The short service should clear the net by about 1 to 18 inches, and it requires little follow-through. Aiming for either corner of the opponent's service area is considered good strategy. Refer to Fig. 3-5 and 3-6 for flight patterns.

Doubles Serving Strategy

The server should follow his service into the court area nearest the net. This procedure prevents confusion as to which player is to take the short return. The server's partner then covers the back area of the court (the *up-and-back* formation). However, if the shuttlecock is high in the opponent's court, giving the opponent an opportunity to execute a smash, the server who is now nearer the net should drop back in the *side-by-side* formation with his partner to prevent their opponents from hitting a smash in between them. If the opponent does hit a smash and it is returned, then one player should move back to the net area and one remain in the back court.

Singles Serving Strategy

The long high serve is used most often in singles. However, it may also be used deceptively in doubles. The execution of the short low service is similar to the execution of the long high service, the difference being that the long high service requires more force and power. The flight pattern of the long high service should be such that the shuttlecock lands near the back boundary line in a singles match and near the long service line in a doubles match.

The Clear

See Fig. 3-7 for stroking techniques. Clear shots may be categorized under three headings. Each heading gets its name from the reason or playing situation that prompts that kind of shot.

When hitting any of the three types of clears:

1. Assume the correct grip. The forehand grip is used at all times except when hitting an underhand clear on the backhand side.

2. Be alert and use correct footwork when hitting the shuttlecock. For example, for clears hit anywhere on the right side of the body, the left shoulder should be toward the net. Reverse this for shots on the left side of the body.

3. Return to playing or ready position after hitting each shot.

The *attacking clear* is hit with the forehand grip, with the racket fully extended over the head. It is an offensive shot that barely goes over or "clears" the opponent's head. See Fig. 3-5 for the flight pattern. In preparation for hitting the attacking clear, the racket is swung back behind the head as you move into position. The movement is similar to the service or overhead smash in tennis, the cracking of a bull whip, or the overhand pitch in baseball. As the racket is taken behind the head the arm is bent at the elbow. As the shuttlecock descends, the arm is fully extended at the point of

FIGURE 3-7. Overhead clear

contact. The point of contact is *slightly in front of you;* in contrast, the overhead smash is contacted directly above the head. Since power is an important factor, hit the shuttlecock with a flat racket face, which permits optimum force and power. The follow-through on the attacking clear is practically nonexistent. The natural movement of the arm is downward after point of contact, but not for the purpose of directing the flight of the shuttlecock, the purpose of all follow-throughs.

The *defensive clear* is hit higher and deeper. Ideally it will land near the back boundary line. As its name implies, it is utilized in order to give you time to return to a good playing position, after having been forced out of position by a good shot from your opponent. See Fig. 3-5 for its flight pattern. The basic differences between the attacking clear and the defensive clear are that the attacking clear has a flatter arc and less upward angle, and requires less power to hit. The same racket motions and body movements are used to hit the defensive clear as required to hit the attacking clear. See Fig. 3-4 for placement areas.

FIGURE 3-8. Forehand drive

FIGURE 3-9. Backhand drive

The *underhand clear* is considered a more advanced stroke and will be presented in a later section (Fig. 4-6).

The Drives

See Figs. 3-8 and 3-9 for stroking techniques. Just as in tennis, there are forehand and backhand drives in badminton. These hints are fundamental to hitting both the forehand and backhand drives.

1. Assume the ready or playing position.

2. Assume the correct grip.

3. Always remember that the left shoulder is toward the net when you are hitting a forehand and the right shoulder is toward the net when you are hitting a backhand.

4. Remember that the right foot is the lead foot; first it is firmly planted at the point of contact, regardless of where you are on the court or the type of shot you hit. The weight is shifted from the left foot to the right foot. After contact move back to the ready position.

The forehand drive is hit with the forehand grip on the right side of the body. The shot is flat, hard, and hit from a sidearm position. Employ the following guidelines when executing the forehand drive. See Figs. 3-5 and 3-6 for its flight pattern.

1. Assume ready position and correct grip.

2. Pivot toward the right of the body, leading with the left foot.

3. At its farthest point your backswing should find the racket head in the vicinity of your shoulder blades, with your elbow bent.

4. As your arm and racket swing toward the shuttlecock, your body weight is transferred from your right foot to your left.

5. Contact the bird near or in front of your left foot about waist level or higher. Most experts are of the opinion that the wrist snaps when the forehand is hit, but a few propose that it shows more of a rolling or rotating motion. Both contentions are sound, but in any case flexibility is important.

The backhand drive is a flat hard shot hit from the left side of the body. See Figs. 3-5 and 3-6 for flight patterns. Similar guidelines are suggested for hitting the backhand as for the forehand, with these exceptions.

1. Change grips.

2. The elbow is bent and points slightly toward the shuttlecock.

3. The right shoulder is toward the net when contact with the shuttlecock is made.

The forehand and backhand drives are valuable when they are hit correctly. Their most advantageous use will be discussed later in this chapter.

TECHNIQUES AND STRATEGY IN PLAY

Most of us have watched players warm up in tennis, basketball, badminton, and other games. Their form was excellent. They could hit with force and accuracy, and moved beautifully. However, when the actual game began, they seemed like different people. Their *strategy* was not equal to other aspects of their game.

Strategy is the mental plan one employs during actual play. It may be divided into offensive and defensive action. When you are on the offensive, you are in control of the contested point and are hitting attacking powerful shots. When you are on the defensive, your opponent theoretically has hit a shot that has forced you out of playing position and you hit a defensive stroke in hopes of regaining good court position.

Offensive strokes in badminton include: the overhead smash, the round-the-head, the overhead attacking clear, the overhead half smash, the overhead drop shot, the underhand drop shot or hairpin net stroke, the drives, and the block. Defensive strokes include: the underhand clear, the overhead defensive clear, and the underhand flick clear.

Singles

Strategy for the singles games is contingent upon whether you are the receiver or server. See Fig. 3-10 for server's and receiver's positions.

The server. The serve most often used in a singles game is the high deep service, previously described. The shuttlecock should land in the court placement areas described in Fig. 3-4. Occasionally, if it is deceptively employed, you can mix in the low short service if your opponent is slow-moving or is standing deep in the service court. The driven serve may also be used, but must come as a complete surprise if it is to be effective. The server's position during delivery should be near the center line about three feet from the short service line. After delivery, you should assume a position astride the center line and move forward or backward as play dictates.

The receiver. The basic returns of service are diagrammed in Fig. 3-10. The

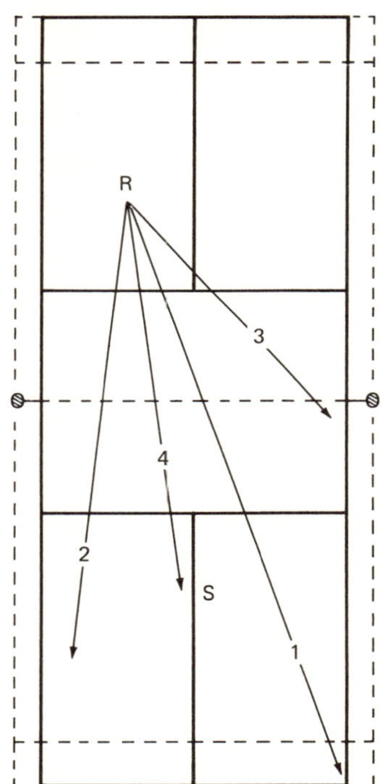

FIGURE 3-10. Return of service in singles. (1) High clear; (2) drive; (3) dropshot; (4) smash.

choice of returns will depend upon whether the service was a short low service or a long high service. The long high service is returned by a high clear to the opponent's backhand, a drop shot either straight down the line or crosscourt, an overhead smash or half-smash, a drive, or an overhead drop shot.

Doubles Formations

There are three basic doubles formations commonly used in a ladies' or men's doubles match. The two most suited for beginners will be discussed in this chapter and a more advanced system will be discussed in a later chapter. In addition, formations for mixed doubles will be suggested. Refer to Fig. 3-11.

Side-by-side pattern. The most easily understood pattern for doubles play is the *side-by-side pattern*. In this formation each player is responsible for half of one side of the court.

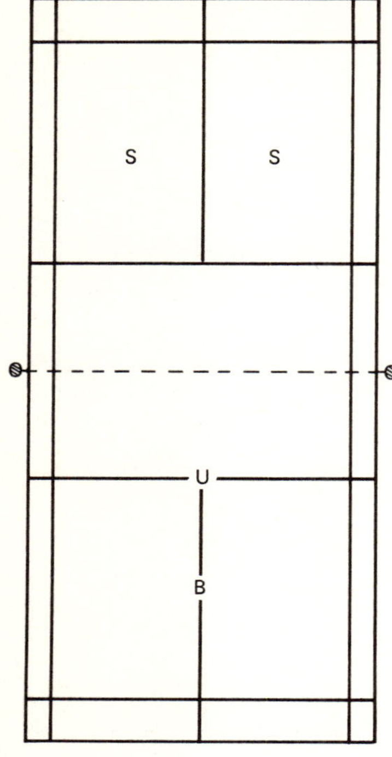

FIGURE 3-11. Doubles formations: side-by-side and up-and-back.

Up-and-back. In this formation, one player takes all the shots in the area closest to the net and one player takes all the shots that are hit in the remaining area of the court.

The server in doubles. See Fig. 3-12 for server's and receiver's positions. The short low service is generally used during a doubles game, but occasionally the driven serve, if deceptively employed, can be very effective. The long high service is less frequently used. See Fig. 3-4 for court placement areas.

The receiver in doubles. The best returns for the short low service include: a drop shot crosscourt or straight down the line, low and out of reach of your opponent who is at the net; a drive; or a high clear to your opponent's backhand (see Fig. 3-10). If the serve is high and deep toward the long doubles service line, a high clear is suggested.

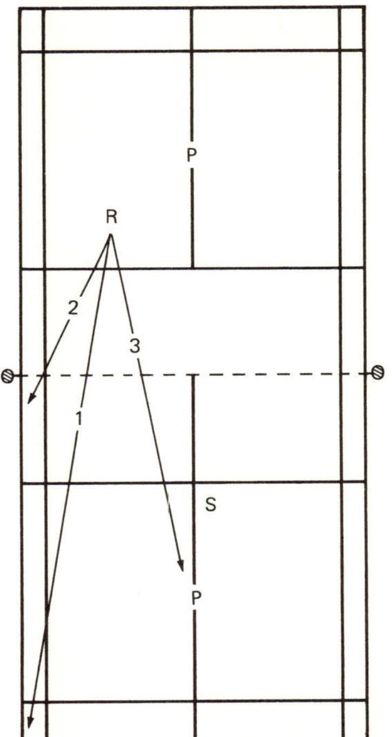

FIGURE 3-12. Return of service in doubles.
(1) High clear; (2) dropshot; (3) drive.

SUMMARY

A great many players use different grips for the backhand and forehand shots. However, the same grip may be used for all shots in badminton.

Court orientation and returning to the playing or ready position is important. Pay careful attention to proper footwork; e.g., when you execute a forehand drive, the right shoulder and right side of the body are slightly or completely parallel to the net.

The follow-through after contacting the shuttlecock is important because it influences direction and helps bring the body back into a natural playing position.

Even though some authorities do not agree that the forehand and backhand drives are beginner's strokes, the following strokes are suggested for beginners: low short service, high deep service, attacking and defensive clear shots, and forehand and backhand drives.

Emphasis on the development of specific skills should go along with the development of sound techniques and strategy in actual play situations.

4

INTRODUCTION TO BADMINTON
history and philosophy

*After having completed this chapter you should understand
the following:*
*1. The importance of studying the history of the
development of sports and games in general, and the
history of badminton specifically*
*2. The chronological development of badminton and
important competitions*
*3. The basic philosophic theories relative to play
and performance*
*4. Your ability to analyze critically the reasons
for your involvement in the game of badminton*

THE HISTORY OF BADMINTON

Historians have provided us with a very accurate account of the
development, achievements, and involvements of mankind throughout civilization. It is usually an exciting experience to identify
with the elements of history, hence our consideration of the history of the game of badminton. This excitement comes from
gaining insight into the times, places, and events that reveal living
performances by individuals. Physical education, involving the
playing of games, has also been accorded a place in historical
documents. Most sports historians will agree that evidence of action of some nature involving the human body is discernible in

33

most accounts of mankind. The term *physical education* was not used before the nineteenth century, though of course games were a part of man's life long before then.

It is often difficult to trace the historical development of a particular game as it is played in our contemporary society. However, most sports historians agree that badminton as it is now played developed from a similar game played in China and Siam. This game was referred to as *battledore* or *shuttlecock*. The game was further developed in India and was called *poona*. Noticeable gaps appear in the historical accounts of the game, but authoritative sources reveal that after certain British officials witnessed the playing of the game in India, they introduced it in England. It received the name of *badminton* because a duke played it at his country estate, known as Badminton. The following dates should be of interest to the player who wishes to establish the chronological history of badminton.

The first record of a similar game was over 2000 years ago in China and Siam.

1873   The game was introduced in England and acquired the name badminton.

1873   The first Badminton Club was formed in Bath, England.

1890s   Badminton was introduced in the United States and Canada.

1895   The National Badminton Association was formed in the United States.

1899   The first All-England Championship for men was played in England. This is the oldest and most famous badminton tournament in the world.

1900   The first Women's Championships were conducted.

1931   The Canadian Badminton Association was founded.

1934   The International Badminton Federation was founded.

1936   The American Badminton Association was founded.

1937   The First United States Championships were conducted.

1948   The Thomas Cup, symbolizing international supremacy of team competition for men, was established. Competition is triennial, with Malaya and Indonesia the usual winners.

1957   The Uber Cup was established as the symbol of international supremacy among women players. The United States has been the consistent winner. Competition is also triennial.

Badminton was not widely played in the United States until the 1930s.

However, United States men have usually placed among the top four teams in the Thomas Cup Competition and the United States women players have dominated the Uber Cup Championships. From this impetus the popularity of the game has spread. Numerous clubs have appeared and a larger number of tournaments are being conducted in private clubs and through the intramural and intercollegiate programs at schools and colleges. In addition, badminton's coeducational appeal as a social and family activity has made it a game enjoyed and played by millions of people of all ages.

PHILOSOPHICAL CONSIDERATIONS

Philosophy, for our purpose, may be defined as practical wisdom that provides fundamental ideas relative to a given topic or activity. Attempts to define the word "play" have produced a variety of responses. Most of the disagreement is a direct result of the many situations to which the word is applied. For us, these fundamental statements seem applicable. Play is an action that involves a direct conscious motive. It involves the individual psychologically and physiologically. It involves individuals of all ages. In essence, play is an essential element in life, and in some instances play may represent life itself. Even though the term play once connoted mere frivolity, contemporary society now views organized play as containing educational substance. Play is recognized as a medium by which one may more nearly reach his potential as a human being and come closer to living the best life possible.

Participation in the game of badminton represents a form of play which is in reality activity with intrinsic rewards. As you play or perform you express yourself, thereby becoming a mentally and physically fit individual. Hence, play is actually a tool by which you can recreate your potential for healthy existence.

AS YOU APPROACH THE GAME OF BADMINTON, THEREFORE, REMEMBER THAT:

Study of the history of a sport gives one an opportunity to gain insights into the perspective of time, places, and events that reveal living performances by individuals.

Sport and games have always been an inherent part of man's physical involvement in life.

Play, properly perceived, is an essential element in life.

PART

II

One Step Further

5

BENEFITS OF BADMINTON

This chapter will discuss the following
benefits of playing badminton, along with
the limitations:
1. Social benefits
2. Psychological benefits
3. Physiological values

Where possible, research to support certain claims will be cited; however, admittedly the major portion of the material presented will be speculative in nature, but educationally sound and logical.

Each of the three areas mentioned demands far more elaboration than space permits. Values or benefits resulting from participation in badminton are tremendously influenced by the conditions under which you are playing, e.g., at a recreation center, with your family, in an organized class situation, or in a championship tournament. Additional factors include: time, purpose or goals, equipment and facilities, instruction, and duration of involvement.

SOCIAL BENEFITS

Broadly defined, the social benefits of badminton include an increase of desirable social traits and experiences, which are a direct result of participation in badminton. You can observe that badminton is fun to play. It can be played by all age groups, family groups, by males and females together, and at all levels of competition. It provides an opportunity to practice good sportsmanship, self-discipline, and control of emotions in a variety of situations, and offers opportunity for physical and verbal interchange. All of these factors are part of social interaction.

Specifically, according to Cratty (1967), man is usually motivated to engage in physical activity by some force within his social structure. You may play badminton because you like the game, because your father plays it, because your best friend or friends play it, because you are conditioned to play through a school or club program, or because your best girlfriend or boyfriend enjoys the game.

If your experience is successful, in one of the aforementioned playing situations you will be satisfied and happy. If not, then social stress and anxiety will no doubt appear. The amount of distress and anxiety is closely related to your goal or reason for playing badminton, the audience, and your opponent.

Physical skills are an additional means, particularly among males, by which social success is measured. Throughout maturation, evidenced proficiencies in performance may exert either a negative or positive influence upon the sociality of the individual.

Personally accepted norms of behavior are formulated, based upon feedback from groups and individuals, as you make perceptions about your performance. These perceptions will influence your selection of activities and the intensity with which you undertake the task.

That physical activity improves social adjustment is a common claim made by physical educators. At best, if participation in a physical activity is to influence an individual's social adjustment favorably, situations involving actual performance will have to be carefully planned with social objectives in mind.

It seems defensible to state that individuals and groups do affect one another's performance. Individual factors such as appearance, aspiration level, competition, personality, leadership qualities, level of skill, body type, maturation level, and audience all bear heavily upon physical performance. An imbalance of either of these individual qualities markedly affects positive or negative social attitudes.

Thus when talking about participation in badminton as a medium for socialization, according to Kenyon (1968), "we must distinguish between the learning of particular roles associated with involvement in sport and physical activity and the learning of a more diffuse role" such as becoming a "democratic citizen" or "well-adjusted" or socially acceptable person.

Even though there is at present little evidence to support the contention that participation in a physical activity is a particularly effective socialization agent, playing badminton does provide an opportunity for social interaction.

Hopefully, this interaction will produce positive affects upon one's "social being."

PSYCHOLOGICAL BENEFITS

Why does a person participate in sports? Whatever these reasons or motivating factors, they help to formulate a personal set of beliefs or a personal philosophy which in turn affects the individual's psychological outlook toward physical activity as well as his potential for psychological benefits from physical activity.

Cofer and Johnson (see page 39) report these theories of motivation: (1) Human motivation is explicable on the basis of unconscious forces, and the resulting behavior is undertaken to resolve conflicts, (2) motivation is built on primary drives through learning on the basis of law of effect and that drive is an energy factor in behavior rather than the determinant of what the individual actually does, (3) human motivation originates from the individual's basic needs such as to explore, to manipulate, and to solve problems, and (4) human motivation, once past the "need" stage, takes on a more specialized appearance and the individual then strives in one area, e.g. sports. Even though it is often accurately claimed that this striving in sports is to compensate for inadequacies, release tensions, or supply an outlet for aggression, engaging in sports is often an end in itself.

Available research seems to indicate that the emphasis on self-actualization dictates that among the needs common to man is the need to be active. Maslow (see 1968) includes in his hierarchy of human needs psychological health and full satisfaction in life. He too proposes that the need for self-actualization or the need to become what one's potential permits is a fundamental. In addition, he proposes that there are appropriate ways of acquiring this state of self-actualization. He theorizes that the self-actualized man is motivated by goals arising from personal growth and applies this assumption to sport. Hence, man should participate in sports because of an intelligent awareness of his needs instead of superficial motives such as money, status, narcissism, and fame.

Johnson (1968) further reports that Layman is of the opinion that the following statements appear to be supported by research evidence. The following is a summary of Layman's statements.

1. There is a close relationship between organic health and personality adjustment. Physical activity and sports contribute positively to the attainment and maintenance of organic health.

2. The acquisition of a motor skill has been found to contribute toward the meeting of basic psychological needs involving safety and self-esteem. However, if the individual is endowed with a low aptitude to learn a specific skill the results may be harmful and feelings of inferiority and insecurity will be produced.

3. Participation in various sports activities positively affects good social adjustment.

4. Improved adjustment when therapy is needed may result from recreational activities.

5. Sports activity provides a healthy outlet for emotions.

6. Under certain conditions, competitive situations may enhance learning and the acquisition of desirable personality traits.

7. Sports activities may provide a setting which is favorable to the development of discriminating values and acceptable ethical character traits.

Badminton is an activity that provides one emotional outlet, one kind of positive experience that may contribute to the fulfillment of certain basic psychological needs.

PHYSIOLOGICAL BENEFITS

The physiological benefits of activity might be thought of as improvements in vital bodily functions. One immediately thinks of how such improvements are reflected in physical fitness, which is one important aspect of total fitness. Extensive research studies dealing with aspects of physiology of badminton players are almost nonexistent. However, there are some studies that concern the effects of exercise per se on the vital organs. In a report by a joint committee of the AMA and the AAHPER (Johnson, 1958), it is stated that one's top physiological limits are greatly influenced by inheritance. However, the extent to which the individual reaches his potential for fitness is dependent upon his exercise habits.

Hunsicker (1958) reported that badminton ranked *high* on a four-point scale as contributing to the physical fitness of an individual.

Based on careful analysis of research and empirical evidence, Steinhaus (1963) concludes that singles badminton rates as a very good cardiovascular conditioner. In a similar rating list, Updyke and Johnson (1970) concur with the cardiovascular benefit and indicate that singles badminton contributes somewhat to muscular endurance. Doubles competition considerably reduces the cardiovascular benefit. Heart rate studies (Kozar and Hunsicker, 1963;

Skubic and Hodgkins, 1967) add support to the cardiovascular value of badminton. These studies indicate that during singles badminton, peak and average heart rates in men and women are in the range of 135 to 160 beats per minute. Based on this evidence as applied to the results of a study by Sharkey and Holleman (1967), we can conclude that if one completes in singles badminton at least three times per week, he can reasonably expect significant improvement in his cardiovascular fitness.

In conclusion, it is important to remember that individuals differ in their capacity to benefit from participation in a vigorous game such as badminton because of variations in body size, strength, structure, all-round athletic ability, psychological attitudes, and differences in present motives and level of competition. However, regular participation in vigorous games of singles badminton may contribute to the attainment and maintenance of a high level of physical fitness, especially the cardiovascular and muscular endurance components.

YOU SHOULD NOW REALIZE THAT:

Participation in badminton, under ideal conditions, may produce increased physiological efficiency, improved social competencies, and desirable psychological reactions on the part of individuals.

Specifically, man is usually inherently motivated to participate in some activity, and sports, including badminton, are an important outlet.

Individuals differ in their capacity to benefit from participation in physical activity owing to the variations in physical and psychological characteristics.

6

BEYOND BASIC SKILLS

This chapter explains the following aspects
of the advanced game:
1. Advanced shots
2. The driven service
3. Advanced techniques of net play and strategy
4. Fitness and conditioning
5. Basic mechanical concepts and movement analysis
6. Basic learning theories applied to badminton

These strokes will add finesse and polish your game, increase your offensive ability, and increase the sheer enjoyment of a faster, more powerful game.

ADVANCED SKILLS

The Round-the-Head Shot

This shot is performed with the forehand grip. By stepping to the left one or two steps in order to move under and closer to the shuttlecock, you can hit a harder, more forceful shot than the backhand drive that you would ordinarily hit. The round-the-head shot may result in a clear, a drop shot, or a half-smash. This stroke is executed in much the same manner as other overhead strokes, with the exception that the shuttlecock is contacted directly above the left shoulder. The arm is fully extended at point of contact and the wrist snaps in a downward motion as you follow through across the right side of the body. This is one of

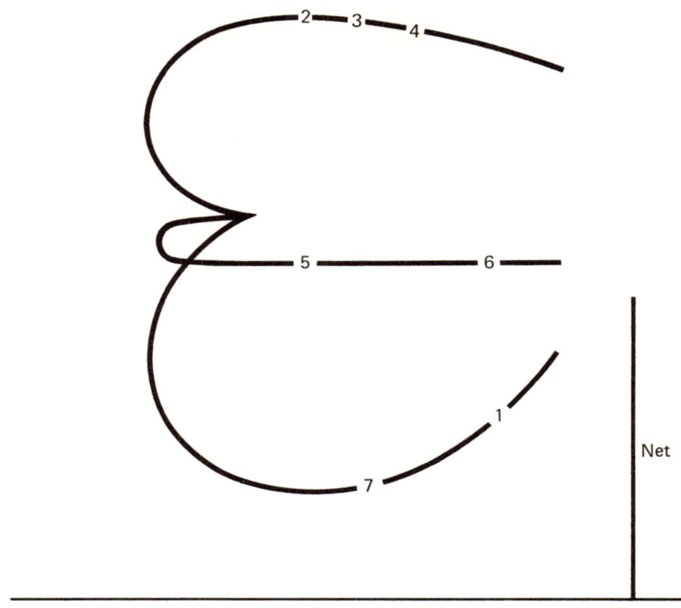

FIGURE 6-1. Points of contact. There may be a range of individual variance. (1) Serve; (2) smash; (3) clear; (4) overhead dropshot; (5) drive; (6) block; (7) underhand clear.

the few times when you are facing the net when hitting a stroke. It is noted that the weight is on the left foot at point of contact and the right foot swings through or forward after contact. See Fig. 6-2 for stroking technique.

The Driven Service

The driven service is most frequently used in doubles. The basic principles outlined in Chapter 3 for the service are essential in performing the driven service. The key difference between the driven service and the low or high service is that with the former the wrist is forcefully flicked in order to give increased speed to the shuttlecock. You want to contact the shuttlecock as high as possible without executing an illegal shot in order to decrease the arc of the flight. Deceptive wrist action (i.e., whether the wrist is locked and rigid, or flexible), the court angle speed, force, and height of the shuttlecock are advantages of the driven service.

FIGURE 6-2. Round-the-head

Net Play

The following discussion presents the advanced techniques and skills required to play at the net position and will be discussed under the general heading of net play. Net play is usually confined to the area between the short service line and the net.

The hairpin shot. This stroke can be performed only when you are within 2 or 3 feet of the net. It may be executed from both the backhand and forehand sides of the body. Sound principles of footwork, grips, and body position applicable to the basic forehand and backhand drives are employed. It is important to loosen the firmness of the grip as you do when hitting the underhand dropshot. Oftentimes you may be facing the net upon actual contact because you are close to the net and because you must move quickly to hit the shot. Little or no backswing or follow-through is required, and the racket face must be flat and facing upward, since your point of contact is below the level of the net.

If you can imagine an inverted hairpin straddling the net, you will be able to visualize the precise flight pattern. It is important that the shuttlecock not go higher than 12 to 18", or your opponent may be able to block or smash your return. See Fig. 4-5 for flight pattern.

The block. This shot is sometimes referred to as a "push" shot, since there is little or no backswing and a very short follow-through. It is usually hit during a doubles game when one player is very close to the net. The forehand grip is used. The shuttlecock must be higher than net level, but is usually not high enough for a full smash. The intent of the block is to force the shuttlecock directly downward near the net in the opponents' court or between the opponents.

The drop shot. The drop shot is a finesse shot that just barely clears the net and falls into the opponent's court.

The underhand drop shot is hit when you are close to the net; on a return of service, it may be hit from the right or left side of the body. See Fig. 4-6 for flight pattern. The footwork, grips, body positions, and transfer of weight are identical to those of the forehand and backhand drives. The key differences between the drop shot and the drives are that the backswing and follow-through on the drop shot are practically nonexistent; the racket is held loosely on the drop shot; the face of the racket is tilted slightly upward to make sure the shuttlecock clears the net; and the power or force is not an essential factor for success with the drop shot.

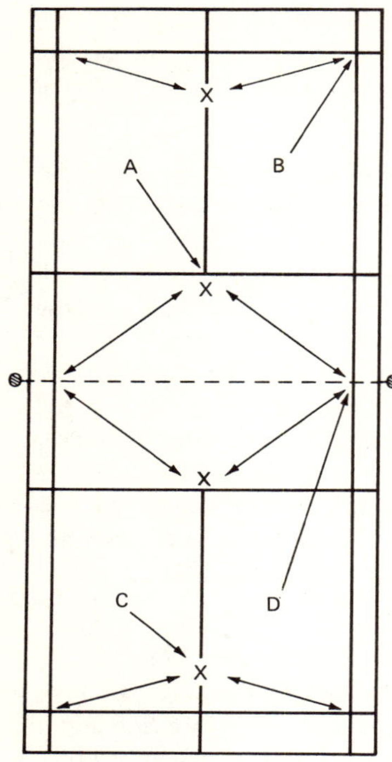

FIGURE 6-3. Patterns of movement for drop and clear drill. The following sequence of movement is suggested in order to provide a sound pattern of movement for practicing dropshots and clears, while improving physical fitness. Follow the direction of the arrows. (1) A begins with a crosscourt dropshot to D. D hits high down-the-line clear to B. A and D move to X position. (2) B clears crosscourt to C. B moves back to X position. (3) C hits crosscourt dropshot to A who clears down-the-line to C. A moves to X position. (4) C hits crosscourt dropshot to A who counters with a dropshot to D. (5) D hits down-the-line clear to B who hits a crosscourt dropshot to D. Repeat this pattern until you can move freely and without hesitation.

The overhead drop shot. The overhead drop shot is a slow shot hit deceptively, employing the exact positioning, backswing, grips, footwork, and arm and wrist movement as described for the overhead clear. See Fig. 4-5 for flight pattern. These are the important differences between the overhead drop shot and the overhead clear:

1. Hit the shuttlecock with a fully extended arm.

2. Contact the shuttlecock farther ahead of the body, with the face of the racket tilted downward in the direction you wish to hit the shuttlecock.

3. All movement prior to contact of the shuttlecock should resemble the smash. At point of contact, little force is applied.

Remember, the overhead drop shot is also a finesse shot and should be stroked with little force. See Fig. 6-4 for stroking techniques.

FIGURE 6-4. Overhead dropshot

FIGURE 6-5. Smash

The smash. The smash or overhead smash is a shot used to "kill" or "put away" any shot higher than the level of the net and higher than the extended arm and racket. See Fig. 4-4 for court placement and Fig. 3-6 for flight pattern. Identical grips, footwork, body position, and backswing are used for the overhead smash, clear, and overhead drop shot. The following differences between the smash and these other shots, and hints for hitting a smash, are suggested.

1. Move into position quickly.

2. Flex or bend the knees slightly.

3. When hitting a smash, keep the right shoulder back and the left shoulder toward the net.

4. Cock the arm and wrist behind the body.

5. Grip the racket firmly.

6. Contact the shuttlecock directly overhead at the highest extension of the racket and arm.

7. Follow through down across the body to the left.

8. Snap the wrist at the point of contact. This puts the face of the racket at a downward angle and causes the shuttlecock to come sharply down into the opponent's court. See Fig. 6-5 for stroking technique.

HINTS FOR ADVANCED STRATEGY IN SINGLES

1. Anticipate returns quickly.

2. Attempt to play the shuttlecock well in front of you, except on the smash. If the shuttlecock passes either side or over your head it is extremely difficult to retrieve.

3. Vary your strokes and pace in order to keep your opponent guessing.

4. Capitalize upon your opponent's weaknesses.

5. Assume and maintain the offensive by planning ahead, by keeping good court position, by hitting accurate, well-placed strokes, and by employing a variety of deceptive strokes.

HINTS FOR ADVANCED STRATEGY IN DOUBLES

The formation used while playing doubles is the key to advanced play. Now that you are familiar with the *side-by-side* and the *up-and-back* formations, you should learn the following systems of play.

The *combination* formation is, as its name suggests, a combination of two systems. The *side-by-side* system is used when your team is on the defense. You and your partner should be near the back boundary line. The *up-and-back* system is used when you are on the offensive. One member of your team covers the territory near the net while the other member covers the backcourt area. See Fig. 4-12.

A fourth system, considered by many to be the best for advanced players, is the *rotation* system. Team members circle counterclockwise. The player in the right side of the court advances to the net. The partner moves into his court area and contacts the shuttlecock with a forehand or stroke on the right side of the body. The players continue to circle, and can hit most shots on the right side of the body. However, many players find this system confusing, and it is most used by high-ranking players.

These general hints should greatly improve your doubles game.

1. When the shuttlecock is high in your opponent's court, that is, when your opponent is in a position to smash, you and your partner should assume the side-by-side position in the backcourt.

2. When either you or your partner has an opportunity to smash, the other should advance to the net to kill the short return of your opponent.

3. Keep most services short and low. Use angled services and occasional high deep services deceptively.

4. Hit most shots down and between your opponents.

5. Assume the offensive as often and as soon as possible. Hit shots that force your opponents to hit up, giving your team a good shot to kill or put away.

6. Keep the shuttlecock in play. Do not make careless errors.

MIXED DOUBLES STRATEGY

Mixed doubles is usually played most often as a social game, but it may be played at a highly competitive level as well. In general, the fundamentals regarding footwork, positioning, and strokes utilized in a regular game of doubles are applicable. Suggestions for successful mixed doubles play include the following:

1. The up-and-back formation is suggested, with the lady usually playing the position closer to the net.

2. The lady should let fast drives and smashes go past her to her partner.

3. The low angled service should be used most often.

4. Returns of service should be low and past the net player, or high, deep clears.

5. The net player, usually the lady, should take all shots within easy reach and hit downward.

6. The man should avoid overprotecting or "hogging" all shots. This makes the game more enjoyable for both players and also makes the man's court area less vulnerable.

CONDITIONING FOR THE GAME

It is very important for you to watch players of high competitive ability before devising your conditioning program. Badminton is often thought of as a delicate game because of the delicate racket, floating shuttlecock, and small court dimensions. If played correctly, however, badminton is a vigorous game demanding power, explosive strength, stamina, and daring.

Fitness or conditioning programs should be purposefully designed for the individual. Fitness involves both the mind and body. This discussion is limited to physical fitness, which is only one aspect of total fitness.

There is scientific evidence to support claims that specially planned physical exercises may favorably affect the body functions. Badminton is one form of vigorous exercise. Badminton is an activity that serves to strengthen various body parts and increase flexibility, skill, speed, and endurance. There should also be included in individual programs a plan by which one relaxes after a practice session or game.

Physical fitness or conditioning to play a vigorous game such as badminton must be attained through the application of sound principles. Exercises and routines that produce high level physical fitness should be applicable to the game itself, if noticeable results are to be attained.

Steinhaus (1963) suggests certain guidelines for the attainment of physical fitness, which are applicable to the attainment of physical conditioning for badminton. In summary, he proposes that one may improve his level of physical fitness by giving attention to these points.

1. Speeding up any movement intensifies it and will develop the muscles in that area more quickly. Therefore, exercises that involve the playing arm and leg muscles are beneficial to the badminton player.

2. Application of a prescribed weight to the muscle area involved in this case, the upper body regions, may speed up the development of strength, power, and endurance.

It is difficult to prescribe a program suited to each individual. However, a well-balanced diet and adequate rest are requisites of any sound conditioning program. A thorough physical examination should precede an increase in physical activity, which involves a strenuous overload on the body systems. A logical rate of increased activity should be planned to prevent harmful exhaustion and muscle stress.

Specifically, if one is free from physical defects or handicaps of any bodily system, alternate running, sprinting, and brisk walking is a tremendous aid in

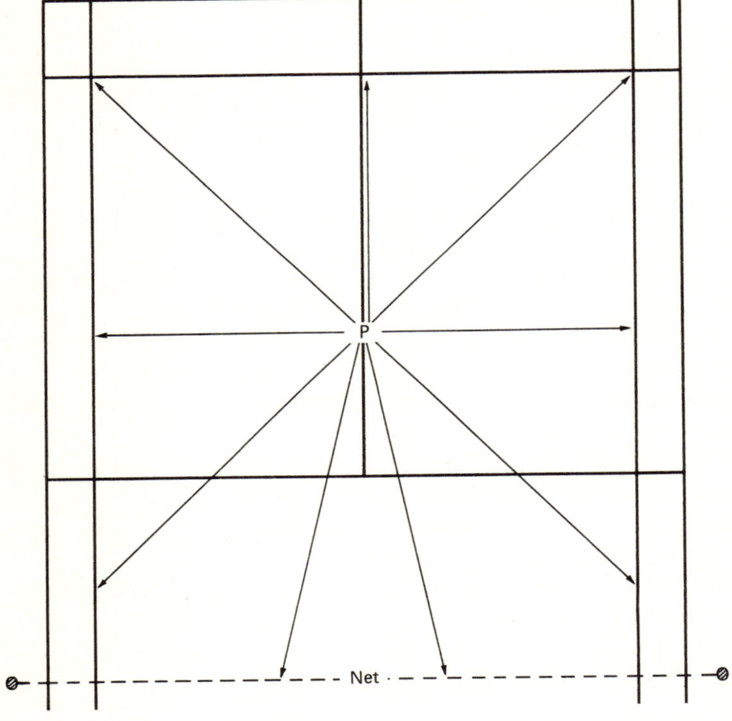

FIGURE 6-6. Drills for improvement of movement patterns and physical conditioning. Note: After each movement, return to the playing position indicated by the letter P. The arrow indicates the direction you move in after you have pivoted from your playing boxing. Concentrate on positioning, footwork, balance. Conditioning will be an added feature if you prolong your time. (2) Move with an opponent hitting the shots to the various court areas. (3) Adjust your movements to the doubles playing situation.

attaining the kind of physical fitness most essential for playing an effective game of badminton.

It is recommended that you repeat this cycle for the development of endurance. Sit-ups, which develop your abdominal muscles, squat-thrusts, which improve strength and agility, and pushups (modified for women), which develop strength in your upper body region, are also suggested.

Additional self-devised exercises are those commonly used in other athletic competitions, such as bouncing on the balls of your feet while your arms are extended overhead, lunging and bending while imitating actual play motions, and rope jumping. Appropriate calisthenics are of value in attaining flexibility, muscle tone, and overall muscle functioning. It is important to remember that the exercises and routines of most value are those that will be utilized during the actual playing situation. Fig. 6-6 illustrates one such exercise, which is suggested as a highly desirable means of attaining and maintaining a high level of physical fitness for badminton. All movements are to be performed realistically.

Over and beyond your sound conditioning program, it is imperative that you maintain a healthy emotional attitude. As one develops his strength, endurance, agility, and coordination, he should also be developing his power of spirit and poise. It is an established fact that one's physical capacity to perform usually exceeds his psychological output, hence a continued healthy mental framework is essential to the physically fit person.

BASIC MECHANICAL CONCEPTS AND MOVEMENT ANALYSIS

The precise basic mechanics involved in movement and performance of a refined motor skill such as playing badminton cannot be described briefly, because the physiological, psychological and social aspects of the individual are all involved. Motivational factors, mental and physical levels of maturation, and motor educability bear heavily upon performance and are largely responsible for the wide variety in skill performance. The following discussion is therefore brief, but hopefully adequate.

The anatomic starting position is considered the fundamental body position in playing badminton. In this position, the feet are comfortably spread and the arms hang by the side, palms toward the body. After the player takes the racket in hand, he bends his knees slightly. The center of gravity or the area of the body where the weight is concentrated is located in the pelvic region.

It is important to remember that the body position must be one from which quick, natural movement can be initiated. This means that, in contrast to the stable, "spread out," low center-of-gravity position of the football player meeting a charge, you want to reduce somewhat the area of the base of support and raise the center of gravity so that a small displacement of the center of gravity will result in quicker movement. Therefore, the feet should *not* be planted too far apart, and the knees should be bent only slightly so that the center of gravity is kept as high as is comfortable.

Movement is a form of force. Force can be felt, its effect can be seen and measured. In badminton force or dynamic application of strength through power is easily felt and observed in hitting the drive or smash. In contrast the almost nonexistent force applied when hitting a finesse or touch shot such as the drop shot can also be felt and observed.

A sound basis for the development of refined motor skill is highly essential. Wells (see page **57**) theorizes that the ability to recognize the elements of a skillful performance precedes skill. She identifies the following characteristics as important in skill.

Efficient Motion

Efficiency in motion is actually expressed in the amount of work accomplished and the energy expended. Beginning badminton players who are poorly coordinated or who do not gain sufficient instruction will make superfluous movements and tend to have unnecessary tensions. The correct application of force on the body regions and muscle areas involved in playing badminton will result in what is called differential relaxation, i.e., the ability to relax unneeded muscles while playing.

Accuracy

Accuracy is a culmination of good mental planning, court orientation (the court positions of you and your opponent), the direction or flight pattern of the shuttlecock, distance, force, timing and muscular reaction, strength, speed, and power.

In addition to the aforementioned requisites of skillful performance, special aptitudes that make for an individual's success in a given sport greatly influence achievement. These special aptitudes include physical proportions, temperament and general mental constitution, and innate athletic characteristics. These include eye-hand coordination, speed, flexibility, and intuitive reflexes. Since the movement involved in the game of badminton is centered around the upper extremities of the body the following factors additionally influence one's level of skill: eye-hand coordination, reaction time, flexibility of the wrist, and peripheral vision.

If your goal is to become the best badminton player that your potential permits, you will want to understand both the anatomical and mechanical principles of human motion.

The following anatomic principles of skilled motion proposed by Wells are applicable to playing badminton.

1. The range of motion may be limited by tight muscles, but may be increased by stretching the tissues involved. This stretching should be preceded by warmup exercises done gradually.

2. The flexibility of weight-bearing joints should not exceed the ability to maintain body regions in good alignment.

3. Unnecessary movements and tensions during performance will result in awkwardness and fatigue.

The following mechanical principles (Broer, 1966) may aid your understanding and performance.

1. The badminton racket has little potential force because it is a relatively light striking implement but this is compensated for by the use of the wrist snap at the moment of impact. This snap, if effective, propels the racket through a long distance very quickly. Wrist flexibility and strength of the small wrist flexor muscles are therefore essential to the power strokes in badminton.

2. Air resistance affects the flight of the shuttlecock more than in other games in which balls are used because of the light weight and the shape of the shuttlecock. Thus, the shuttle falls more slowly than the tennis ball and does not follow the same parabolic path. This often causes the beginner to misjudge the flight of the cock or swing too early.

LEARNING THEORIES APPLIED TO BADMINTON

The following discussion is based on theories of motor learning prepared by Cratty (1967). Motor learning, as you recall, we defined as a change in the level of skill.

Specific theoretical assumptions relevant to learning to play badminton include:

1. "Thinking through" a movement facilitates the learning of complex motor skills.

2. Skillful performance of a special technique is achieved only through practicing the technique.

3. Kinesthetic perception (awareness of the body in space and the relationships among the body parts) is an important factor in learning and perfecting motor skills.

4. Overpractice may diminish skillful performance and decrease motivation.

5. Learning a motor skill may be facilitated by application of the theory of *reinforcement* and the "contiguity theory." Reinforcement, basically, consists of a "reward" for correct performance, and should come during the actual practice of a skill. Examples of types of reinforcement "rewards" are: winning a match, attaining a high score on a particular skills test, or a verbal reward from an observer. The "contiguity theory" is based upon the concept that learning occurs when a stimulus (a match) and a response (good play) occur simultaneously.

6. Learners who are quick to acquire a new skill and who perform well in several activities usually exemplify several of these characteristics: a high degree of motivation, above average strength, ability to analyze the mechanics of a task accurately and rapidly, and freedom from unnecessary tensions, which impede performance.

7. Massing of practice results in greater learning, because each performance places the forgetting curve of the previous performance at a higher level.

Generally speaking, the nature or purpose of the task dictates whether *whole, part,* or *progressive-part* practice is the most efficient means of learning. Most educators agree that the limit of the learner's perceptual span largely determines the degree to which the "whole" of the task is presented. Further, spacing practice seems to facilitate the learning of motor skills, through offsetting fatigue and preventing boredom.

The following generalizations concerning instruction are applicable to learning to play badminton.

Instruction may be one of three types: self-instruction, instruction from another person, and instruction from the task itself. All instruction occurs in three stages: pre-performance, actual performance, and post-performance or evaluation.

Available literature on skill performance proposes that pre-performance instruction should be a combination of verbal, visual demonstration, written material, and manual guidance. Instruction during performance should not interfere with the learner's focus upon the movement pattern. Evaluative instruction should point out both failures and successes. Direction emphasizing the correct way of performing a skill is considered more profitable than emphasizing the incorrect way.

Teaching and learning have always been an integral part of mankind's existence. Learning to play badminton is a part of this exciting atmosphere and offers a distinct challenge to your physical and mental prowess.

EVALUATION OF ACHIEVEMENT

In order for any learning experience to be meaningful, the results must be measured. It is difficult to determine the rate at which your game will improve because so many factors are involved: your goals and playing ability, the nature of the instruction, and frequency of practice and play. However, when you arrive at a point where you desire evaluation, you may measure your achievement in the following ways.

Stroke Production

I would suggest that as you evaluate yourself or as you are evaluated by another person, one main principle be applied. Can you successfully hit the shuttlecock to the desired court area, at the desired game situation speed and power, and can you do so consistently?

Theoretical or Observation Appraisal

This means of evaluation is sometimes not widely accepted, because it involves subjectivity. However, if the teacher is conscientious and knows the students, this can be a very desirable method of evaluation. It consists of watching the performer play a match or playing against the person being evaluated.

This method of evaluation may be more valid as a means by which an individual may make a self-evaluation of progress because he is actually playing the game while being evaluated. The most important reasons for evaluating by this method are that the individual performer should be able to:

1. Utilize all the rules and laws of the game outside of and during actual play situations.

2. Devise strategy and patterns of play after observation of opponent's strengths and weaknesses.

3. Assess skill in performance in light of opponent's performance.

4. Detect and correct his own weaknesses.

Skill in Performance

Enjoyment of a game is contingent upon execution of the various skills it involves. It is important that you appraise your execution of a specific skill in light of: consistency, or number of times you can accomplish a particular stroke (e.g., can you hit a service 10 consecutive times within 6 to 18" of the top of the net and within 1 to 12" of the short service line?); speed and power commensurate to an actual game situation; court placement and accuracy; performance of skills during a warmup rally and under competitive play conditions.

AS YOU WORK TO IMPROVE YOUR GAME, KEEP IN MIND THAT:

Advanced play requires more strokes and more advanced techniques and patterns of strategy than beginning play does.

Advanced skills include the round-the-head shot, driven service, hairpin shot, block, drop shot (overhead and underhand), and the smash.

Badminton is a game which, if played correctly, demands power, explosive strength, endurance, daring, mental reasoning, agility, and finesse.

To play at your highest potential requires that you design a vigorous conditioning program, and attain and maintain a high level of physical fitness.

A thorough knowledge of the mechanical concepts and analysis of movement enhances a good performance.

The application of basic learning theories to the acquisition of a motor skill is important.

Periodic evaluation of achievement is essential to assess improvement and provide additional motivation for future involvement in the game.

APPENDIX
badminton rules

The basic rules and terminology of a game are essential for all participants. Adherance to rules is a mark of skill in the game. To communicate enjoyably concerning a particular game also requires one to be able to recognize and use essential terms and phrases applicable to the game. In the following section, the exact rules are presented and the basic terminology of badminton is explained. (See also Glossary.) The following laws are quoted verbatim as they appear in the American Badminton Association Handbook.

THE RULES

1. (a) COURT. The court shall be laid out as in Figure 1 and 2 (except in the case provided for in paragraph "B" of this Law) and to the measurements there shown and shall be defined by white, black, or other easily distinguishable lines, 1 1/2 inches wide.

In marking the court, the width (1 1/2 inches) of the center lines shall be equally divided between the right and left service-

Permission to print the official Laws of Badminton was granted by the American Badminton Association with this condition: "Although the following are the rules of this date (1969), these rules may change from year to year to some extent. Hence, anytime after July, 1969, to assure yourself that you are dealing with the up-to-date rules, you should secure them from the Chairman of the American Badminton Association."

courts; the width (1 1/2 inches each) of the short service line and the long service line shall fall within the 13 foot measurement given as the length of the service-court; and the width (1 1/2 inches each) of all other boundary lines shall fall within the measurements given.

(b) Where space does not permit of the marking out of a court for doubles, a court may be marked out for singles only as shown in Figure 2. The back boundary lines become also the long service lines, and the posts, or the strips of material representing them as referred to in Law 2, shall be placed on the side lines.

2. POSTS. The posts shall be 5 feet 1 inch in height from the floor. They shall be sufficiently firm to keep the net strained as provided in Law 3, and shall be placed on the side boundary lines of the court. Where this is not practicable, some method must be employed for indicating the position of the side boundary line where it passes under the net. e.g. by the use of a thin post or strip of material, not less than 1 1/2 inches in width, fixed to the side boundary line and rising vertically to the net cord. Where this is in use on a court marked for doubles it shall be placed on the side boundary line of the doubles court irrespective of whether singles or doubles are being played.

3. NET. The net shall be made of fine tanned cord of 1/4 inch mesh. It shall be firmly stretched from post to post, and shall be 2 feet 6 inches in depth. The top of the net shall be 5 feet in height from the floor at the center, and 5 feet 1 inch at the posts, and shall be edged with a 3 inch white tape doubled and supported by a cord or cable run through the tape and strained over and flush with the top of the posts.

4. SHUTTLE. A shuttle shall weigh from 73 to 85 grains, and shall have from 14 to 16 feathers fixed in a cork, 1 inch to 1 1/8 inches in diameter. The feathers shall be from 2 1/2 to 2 3/4 inches in length from the tip to the top of the cork base. They shall have from 2 1/8 to 2 1/2 inches spread at the top and shall be firmly fastened with thread or other suitable material.

Subject to there being no substantial variation in the general design, pace, weight and flight of the shuttle, modifications in the above specifications may be made, subject to the approval of the National Organization concerned (a) in places where atmospheric conditions, due either to altitude or climate, make the standard shuttle unsuitable; or (b) if special circumstances exist which make it otherwise expedient in the interests of the game.

A shuttle shall be deemed to be of correct pace if, when a player of average strength strikes it with a full underhand stroke from a spot immediately above one back boundary line in a line parallel to the side lines, and at an upward angle, it falls not less than 1 foot, and not more than 2 feet 6 inches, short of the other back boundary line.

5. (a) PLAYERS. The word "Player" applies to all those taking part in a game.

(b) The game shall be played, in the case of the doubles game, by two players a side, and in the case of the singles game, by one player a side.

(c) The side for the time being having the right to serve shall be called the "in" side, and the opposing side shall be called the "out" side.

6. TOSS. Before commencing play the opposing sides shall toss, and the side winning the toss shall have the option of: (a) Serving first; or (b) Not serving first; (c) Choosing ends. The side losing the toss shall then have choice of any alternative remaining.

7. (a) SCORING. The doubles and men's singles game consists of 15 or 21 points, as may be arranged. Provided that in a game of 15 points, when the score is 13 all, the side which first reached 13 has the option of "setting" the game to 5 and that when the score is 14 all, the side which first reached 14 has the option of "setting" the game to 3. After a game has been "set" the score is called "love all," and the side which first scores 5 or 3 points, according as the game has been "set" at 13 or 14 all, wins the game. In either case the claim to "set" the game must be made before the next service is delivered after the socre has reached 13 all or 14 all. Provided also that in a game of 21 points the same method of scoring be adopted, substituting 19 and 20 for 13 and 14.

(b) The ladies' singles game consists of 11 points. Provided that when the score is "9 all" the player who first reached 9 has the option of "setting" the game to 3, and when the score is "10 all" the player who first reached 10 has the option of "setting" the game to 2.

(c) A side rejecting the option of "setting" at first opportunity shall not be thereby debarred from "setting" if a second opportunity arises.

(d) In handicap games "setting" is not permitted.

8. The opposing sides shall contest the best of 3 games, unless otherwise agreed. The players shall change ends at the commencement of the second game and also of the third game (if any). In the third game the players shall change ends when the leading score reaches:

(a) 8 in a game of 15 points;

(b) 6 in a game of 11 points;

(c) 11 in a game of 21 points;

or, in a handicap event, when one of the sides has scored half the total number of points required to win the game (the next highest number being taken in case of fractions). When it has been agreed to play only one game the players shall change ends as provided above for the third game.

If, inadvertently, the players omit to change ends as provided in this Law at the score indicated, the ends shall be changed immediately the mistake is discovered, and the existing score shall stand.

9. (a) DOUBLES PLAY. It having been decided which side is to have the service, the player in the right-hand service-court of that side commences the game by serving to the player in the service-court diagonally opposite. If the latter player returns the shuttle before it touches the ground, it is to be returned by one of the "in" side, and then returned by one of the "out" side, and so on, till a fault is made or the shuttle ceases to be "in play" (see paragraph (b)). If a fault is made by the "in" side, its right to continue serving is lost, as only one player on the side beginning a game is entitled to do so (provided in Law 11), and the opponent in the right-hand service-court then becomes the server; but if the service is not returned, or the fault is made by the "out" side, the "in" side scored a point. The "in" side players then change from one service-court to the other, the service now being from the left-hand service-court to the player in the service-court diagonally opposite. So long as a side remains "in," service is delivered alternately from each service-court into the one diagonally opposite, the change being made by the "in" side when, and only when a point is added to its score.

(b) The first service of a side in each inning shall be made from the right-hand service-court. A "service" is delivered as soon as the shuttle is struck by the server's racket. The shuttle is thereafter "in play" until it touches the ground, or until a fault or "let" occurs, or except as provided in Law 19. After the service is delivered, the server and the player served to may take up any position they choose on their side of the net, irrespective of any boundary lines.

10. The player served to may alone receive the service, but should the shuttle touch, or be struck by, his partner the "in" side scores a point. No player may receive two consecutive services in the same game, except as provided in Law 12.

11. Only one player of the side beginning a game shall be entitled to serve in its first innings. In all subsequent innings, each partner shall have the right, and they shall serve consecutively. The side winning a game shall always serve first in the next game, but either of the winners may serve and either of the losers may receive the service.

12. If a player serves out of turn, or from the wrong service-court (owing to a mistake as to the service-court from which service is at the time being in order), *and his side wins the rally*, it shall be a "let," provided that such "let" be claimed or allowed before the next succeeding service is delivered.

If a player standing in the wrong service-court takes the service *and his side wins the rally*, it shall be a "let" provided that such "let" be claimed or allowed before the next succeeding service is delivered. If in either of the above cases the side at fault loses the rally, the mistake shall stand and the players' position shall not be corrected during the remainder of the game.

Should a player inadvertently change sides when he should not do so and the mistake not be discovered until after the next succeeding service has been delivered, the mistake shall stand, and a "let" cannot be claimed or allowed, and the players' position shall not be corrected during the remainder of that game.

13. SINGLES PLAY. In singles Laws 9 and 12 hold good except that:

(a) The players shall serve from and receive service in their respective right-hand service-courts only when the server's score is 0 or an even number of points in the game, the service being delivered from and received in their respective left-hand service-courts when the server's score is an odd number of points.

(b) Both players shall change service-courts after each point has been scored.

14. FAULTS. A fault made by a player of the side which is "in" puts the server out; if made by a player whose side is "out," it counts a point to the "in" side.

It is a fault:

(a) If in serving, the shuttle at the instant of being struck be higher than the server's waist, or if any part of the head of the racket, at the instant of striking the shuttle, be higher than any part of the server's hand holding the racket.

(b) If, in serving, the shuttle falls into the wrong service-court, (i.e., into the one not diagonally opposite to the server), or falls short of the short service line, or beyond the long service line, or outside the side boundary lines of the service-court into which service is in order.

(c) If the server's feet are not in the service-court from which service is at the time being in order, or if the feet of the player receiving the service are not in the service-court diagonally opposite until the service is delivered. (See Law 16.)

(d) If before or during the delivery of the service any player makes preliminary feints or otherwise intentionally balks his opponent.

(e) If, either in service or play, the shuttle falls outside the boundaries of the court, or passes through or under the net, or fails to pass the net, or touches the roof or side walls, or the person or dress of a player. (A shuttle falling on a line shall be deemed to have fallen in the court or service-court of which such line is a boundary.)

(f) If the shuttle "in play" be struck before it crosses to the striker's side of the net. (The striker may, however, follow the shuttle over the net with his racket in the course of his stroke.)

(g) If, when the shuttle is "in play," a player touches the net or its supports with racket, person or dress.

(h) If the shuttle be held on the racket (i.e. caught or slung) during the execution of a stroke; or if the shuttle be hit twice in succession by the same player with two strokes; or if the shuttle be hit by a player and his partner successively.

(i) If in play a player strikes the shuttle (unless he thereby makes a good return) or is struck by it, whether he is standing within or outside the boundaries of the court.

(j) If a player obstructs an opponent.

(k) If Law 16 be transgressed.

15. GENERAL. The server may not serve till his opponent is ready, but the opponent shall be deemed to be ready if a return of the service be attempted.

16. The server and the player served to must stand within the limits of their respective service-courts (as bounded by the short and long service, the center, and side lines), and some part of both feet of these players must remain in contact with the ground in a stationary position until the service is delivered. A foot on or touching a line in the case of either the server or the receiver shall be held to be outside his service-court (See Law 14 (c)). The respective partners may take up any position, provided they do not unsight or otherwise obstruct an opponent.

17. If the receiver is faulted for moving before service is delivered, or for not being within the correct service court, in accordance with Laws 14 (c) or 16, and at the same time the server is also faulted for a service infringement, it shall be a "let."

18. If the server, in attempting to serve, misses the shuttle, it is not a fault; but if the shuttle be touched by the racket, a service is thereby delivered.

19. If, when in play, the shuttle strikes the net and remains suspended there, or strikes the net and falls towards the ground on the striker's side of the net, or hits the ground outside the court and an opponent then touches the net or shuttle with his racket or person, there is no penalty, as the shuttle is not *then* in play.

20. If a player has a chance of striking the shuttle in a downward direction when quite near the net, his opponent must not put up his racket near the net on the chance of the shuttle rebounding from it.

This is obstruction within the meaning of Law 14 (j).

A player may, however, hold up his racket to protect his face from being hit if he does not thereby balk his opponent.

21. It shall be the duty of the umpire to call "fault" or "let" should either occur, without appeal being made by the players, and to give his decision on any appeal regarding a point in dispute, if made before the next service; and also to appoint linesmen and service judges at his discretion. The umpire's decision shall be final, but he shall uphold the decision of a linesman or service judge. This does not preclude the umpire also from faulting the server or receiver. Where, however, a referee is appointed, an appeal shall lie to him from the decision of an umpire on questions of law only.

22. Play shall be continuous from the first service until the match be concluded: except that (a) in the International Badminton Championships, there shall be allowed an interval not exceeding five minutes between the second and third games of the match; (b) in countries where climatic conditions render it desirable, there shall be allowed, subject to the previously published approval of the National Organization concerned, an interval not exceeding five minutes between the second and third games of a match, in singles or doubles, or both, and (c) when necessitated by circumstances not within the control of the players, the umpire may suspend play for such a period as he may consider necessary. If play be suspended, the existing score shall stand and play be resumed from that point. Under no circumstances shall play be suspended to enable a player to recover his strength or wind, or to receive instruction or advice. Except in the case of any interval already provided for above, no player shall be allowed to leave the court until the match be concluded without the umpire's consent. The umpire shall be the sole judge of any suspension of play and he shall have the right to disqualify an offender.

INTERPRETATIONS

1. Any movement or conduct by the server that has the effect of breaking the continuity of service after the server and receiver have taken their positions to serve and to receive the service is a preliminary feint. (See Law 14 (d)).

2. It is a fault under Law 14 (h) if the shuttle be hit otherwise than by one impact with the racket. But it is not a fault (provided the stroke be otherwise legitimate) (a) if the base and feathers of the shuttle be struck simultaneously, or (b) if the shuttle be struck with one distinct hit only by any part of the racket.

3. It is obstruction if a player invade an opponent's court with racket or person in any degree except as permitted in Law 14 (f). (See Law 14 (j)).

4. Where necessary on account of the structure of a building, the local Badminton Authority may, subject to the right of veto of its National Organization, make by-laws dealing with cases in which a shuttle touches an obstruction.

GLOSSARY OF TERMS

Badminton has some terms that almost defy logic. However, they are an interesting aspect of the game and are necessary for communication with other players.

A.B.A.: The American Badminton Association, which is the national governing body in the United States.

Alley: The space between the side boundary line (for singles) and the boundary line for doubles.

Back Alley: The area between the back boundary line and the long service line. The shuttlecock may not be served into this area during doubles play.

Backcourt: The general area near the back boundary line.

Backhand: A shot made from the left side of the body (for right-handed players).

Balk: A movement that distracts or interferes with an opponent before or during the service. Sometimes referred to as a "feint."

Bird: Nickname for the shuttlecock or shuttle.

Block: Placing the racket in a stationary position so that the shuttle rebounds back into the opponent's side of the net. The block is not a fundamental stroke.

Carry: An incident when the shuttle momentarily remains on the strings during the execution of a stroke. The carry may be referred to as a sling or throw and is illegal.

Center Position: Sometimes referred to as the "basic" playing position in relation to the lines of the court, the opponent and shuttle, and the net.

Change Ends of Court: Players change sides or ends of the court at designated intervals during a match.

Clear: High deep shot, most effective when hit near the back boundary line.

Combination Doubles Formation: Rotation of the side-by-side and the up-and-back doubles formations.

Court: Official area of play.

Crossout Shots: Shots hit diagonally from one side of the court to the other.

Deception: Stroking to catch the opponent off guard, by changing direction and speed of the shuttle at the last minute.

Defense: The situation you are in when your opponent has maneuvered you out of position.

Double Hit: Hitting the shuttle twice in succession on the same stroke. An illegal procedure.

Doubles: A game in which two opponents are on each side of the court.

Down: A hand is down when one person on a team has served and fails to score.

Drive: A fast and low shot that makes a horizontal flight pattern over the net.

Driven Serve: A hard or quickly hit serve with a flat trajectory.

Drop Shot: A touch or finesse stroke hit with very little speed, which falls close to the net on the opponent's side.

Face: The hitting surface of the racket.

Fault: Any violation of the rules. Most faults are broadly classified as either serving or receiving faults, i.e., either the shuttle fails to go over the net or lands outside the specified boundary.

First Service: Normally used in doubles. Denotes that the player serving retains service.

Flat: Level horizontal trajectory of the shuttle. Also, the angle of the face of the racket that does not impart spin to the shuttle.

Flick: A shortened stroke that speeds up the shuttle with a quick wrist action. Useful in stroking from below the level of the net, thereby surprising an opponent by quickly changing a soft shot into a faster passing shot.

Foot Fault: Illegal moving of the foot or stepping on the service line during service.

Forehand: A stroke hit on the right side of the body (right-handed players).

Game: A game unit consists of 15 points in men's singles and in all doubles games and 11 points in ladies' singles, unless the game has been "set."

Game Bird: Game winning point.

Hairpin Net Shot: Stroke made from below and very close to the net with the shuttle just clearing the net and then dropping sharply downward. Takes its name from the shape of the shuttle's flight in a perfectly executed shot.

Halfcourt Shot: Shot placed midcourt. Used more in doubles than in singles play, especially effective against the up-and-back formation.

Head: The stringed end of the racket, which contacts the shuttle.

I.B.F.: International Badminton Federation, the world governing body for badminton. The I.B.F. is governed by an annual meeting of the elected representatives of every national association in membership. One of its many functions is the management of the world famous international team competitions for the Thomas Cup and the Uber Cup.

Inning: Term of Service. Interval of time during which a player or team holds the service.

In Play: The shuttle is considered to be "in play" from the time it is struck by the server's racket until it touches the court or a fault or let occurs. See exception stated in the rules.

In Side: Side having the right to serve.

Kill: Fast downward shot, which usually cannot be returned. Often referred to as a put-away.

Let: An incident where an exchange or rally is replayed. (See official rules for examples.)

Lob: A high shot that goes over the opponent's head.

Love: No score. English pronunciation of the French word "l'oeuf," meaning goose-egg or zero. To start a singles match the umpire calls "love-all, play." To start a doubles match he says "hand out, love-all, play."

Love-All: No score on either side. Also used after a game has been set. (See "setting".)

Match: Best two out of three games.

Match Point: A point, which is won, terminates the match.

Net Shot: Shot hit from the forecourt with the shuttle just clearing the netcord. Hairpin net shots, push shots, and net smashes are the three most popular net shots.

New York Badminton Club: Founded in 1878, it is one of the oldest organized clubs in the world.

No Shot: Badminton procedure requires a player to call "no shot" immediately when he has faulted by carrying, slinging, or throwing the shuttle.

Odd and Even Court: In singles the right half court when facing the net is "even" and the left half is "odd." In doubles the player in the right court is "even" and the player in the left court is "odd."

Offense: The player or team in control or attacking.

Out Side: Side receiving serve.

Passing Shot: A shot that passes to the side of the opponent, not over his head.

Placement: Hitting the shuttle to an advantageous place on the court.

Point: Unit of scoring.

Poona: Some historians believe the original name for badminton was *poona,* from the city of Poona in India, where a badminton-type game was played in the 1860's.

Push Shot: A gentle net shot played by merely pushing the shuttle without force.

Rally: Hitting the shuttle across the net to warm up; an extended exchange of shots during play.

Ready Position: An alert body position enabling quick movement in any direction.

Round-the-Head Shot: Stroke peculiar to badminton. An overhead stroke played on the left side of the body with the forehand grip. The contact point is above the left shoulder.

Rush-the-Serve: Rapid advance to the net in an attempt to put away a high, short serve simply by smashing the shuttle down into an opponent's court. Used mostly in doubles.

Second Service: Normally used in doubles. Indicates that one partner is "down," i.e., he has already had his turn at serving.

Serve, Service: Act of putting the shuttle into play. Opening stroke of each exchange or rally.

Service Court: The area into which the serve must be delivered.

Setting: Method of extending games by increasing the number of points necessary to win tied games. Player reaching tied score first has option of setting. See official rules for explanation of when the score may be set.

Set-Up: Poor shot that makes a winning shot or "kill" easy for the opponent.

Shaft: The part of the racket between the head and the handle.

Short: Failure of the shuttle to reach the desired area of the court.

Shuttlecock: Official name for the shuttle, the object hit over the net.

Side-By-Side: A doubles formation where both players occupy positions parallel to the net.

Side-In-and Side-Out: Refers to the beginning of the service series or the ending of the serving series.

Smash: Hard hit overhead shot that forces the shuttle sharply downward. The chief attacking stroke.

Spin-the-Racket: The racket is spun to determine which player serves first. An identification mark on one side of the racket is selected by one player prior to the spin. If that mark appears after the racket is spun, that player may choose to serve.

Stroke: Action of striking the shuttle with the racket.

Up-and-Back: Popular doubles and mixed doubles formation in which one player is up near the net and the partner is near the back boundary line.

Wood Shot: The shot that results when the base of the shuttle is hit by the frame of the racket rather than by the strings.

SELECTED REFERENCES AND READINGS

Ainsworth, Dorothy, and others, ed. 1963. *Individual sports for women*, 4th ed. Philadelphia: W.B. Saunders Co.

Anselm, Elizabeth. 1958. Plastic shuttlecocks or our feathered friend. *Selected tennis-badminton articles*. DGWS, pp. 78-79.

The Badminton Association of England. *Know the game—badminton*. Box 634, New Rochelle, N.Y.: Sport-Shelf (Distributors).

Bourquardez, Virginia, and Heilman, Charles. 1950. *Sports equipment*. Englewood Cliffs, N.J.: Prentice-Hall, Inc., p. 208.

Broer, M. 1966. *Efficiency of human movement*. Philadelphia: W. B. Saunders Co.

Century-Crofts. 1962. *Values in sports*. Washington, D.C.: American Association for Health, Physical Education and Recreation.

Cratty, Bryant J. 1964. *Movement behavior and motor learning*. Philadelphia: Lea & Febiger, pp. 22-26.

―――― 1968. *Psychology and physical activity*. Englewood Cliffs, N.J.: Prentice-Hall, Inc., pp. 3-25.

―――― 1967. *Social dimensions of physical activity*. Englewood Cliffs, N.J.: Prentice-Hall, Inc., pp. 1-81.

Davidson, Kenneth R. 1951. The shuttlecock. *Bird Chatter*, March-April, p. 7.

Davidson, Kenneth R., and Gustavson, Leland R. 1953. *Winning badminton*. New York: Ronald Press Co.

――――, and Smith, Lenore C. (consultants). *Badminton*. New York: Sterling Publishing Co.

Davis, Dorothy, ed. 1963. *Selected tennis-badminton articles.* 1201-16th St., N.W., Washington, D.C.: DGWS.

Devlin, Mrs. Frank, ed. *Badminton U.S.A.* 2 Dolfield Rd., Owings Mills, Md.

DeWitt, Raymond T. 1953. *Teaching individual and team sports.* Englewood Cliffs, N.J.: Prentice-Hall, Inc.

Dilldall, Robert. 1951. The new plastic shuttle. *Bird Chatter*, March-April, pp. 8-9.

Fait, Hollis P.; Shaw, John H.; Fox, Grace I.; and Hollingsworth, Cecil B. 1961. *A manual of physical education activities,* 2nd ed. Philadelphia: W. B. Saunders Co.

Forgie, Hugh. *You can play badminton.* Cortland, N.Y.: Cortland Racket Division.

Friedrich, John, and Rutledge, Abbie. 1962. *Beginning badminton.* Belmont, Calif.: Wadsworth Publishing Company, Inc.

Hale, Patricia Whitaker. 1956-1958. Design for badminton cart. *Tennis-badminton guide.* DGWS, pp. 94-98.

The hand book of the international badminton federation. 53 Westwood Hill, London S.E. 26, England.

Hooks, Gene. 1962. *Application of weight training to athletics.* Englewood Cliffs, N.J.: Prentice-Hall, Inc.

Hunsicker, Paul. *Physical fitness.* Washington, D.C.: National Education Association, pp. 4-12, 23.

Johnson. 1958. Exercise and fitness. Washington, D.C.: American Association for Health, Physical Education, and Recreation.

Karpovich, Peter V. 1953. *Physiology of muscular activity.* Philadelphia: W. B. Saunders Co., p. 244.

Kenyon, Gerald S. 1968. Sociological consideration. *Journal of Health, Physical Education and Recreation.* Washington, D.C.: American Association for Health, Physical Education, and Recreation, November-December, pp. 31-33.

Kozar, J. J., and Hunsicker, P. 1963. A study of telemetered heart rate during sports participation of young adult men. *Journal of Sports Medicine and Physical Fitness*, 3:1.

Landtroop, Peggy Vilbig. 1958. Kinds of equipment to purchase for school use: its storage and care. *Selected tennis-badminton articles.* DGWS, pp. 76-77.

Lipman, Jacob. 1951. On stringing a racket. *Bird Chatter*, January-February, p. 20.

Miller, Donna Mae, and Ley, Katherine L. 1955. *Individual and team sports for women.* Englewood Cliffs, N.J.: Prentice-Hall, Inc.

Mitchell, Elmer D., ed. 1952. *Sports for recreation—and how to play them*, rev. ed. New York: The Ronald Press Co.

Morgan, William P. 1968. Psychological considerations. *Journal of Health, Physical Education and Recreation*. Washington, D.C.: American Association of Health, Physical Education and Recreation, November-December, p. 27.

—— 1960. Fit for college. Washington, D.C.: American Association of Health, Physical Education and Recreation, p. 5.

Physical education for high school students. 1963. Washington, D.C.: American Association for Health, Physical Education and Recreation.

Poole, James. 1969. *Badminton*. Pacific Palisades, Calif.: Goodyear Publishing Company.

Schelle, H.A.E., ed. *The badminton gazette*. Churchtown, Chislehurst, Kent, England.

Sharkey, B., and Holleman, J. P. 1967. Cardio-respiratory adaptations to training at specific intensities. *Research Quarterly*, 38:698.

Skubic, V., and Hodgkins, J. 1967. Relative strenuousness of selected sports as performed by women. *Research Quarterly*, 38:305.

Steinhaus, A. H. 1963. *How to keep fit and like it*. Chicago: George Williams College.

Steinhaus, A. H. 1963. *Toward a better understanding in health and physical education*. Dubuque, Iowa: Wm. C Brown Co., pp. 63-65.

Thompson, B. P. 1963. Be kind to shuttlecocks. *Bird Chatter*, May-June, p. 11.

Updyke, W. F., and Johnson, P. B. 1970. *Principles of modern physical education, health, and recreation*. New York: Holt, Rinehart and Winston.

Van Dalen, Deobold B. 1953. *A world history of physical education*. Englewood Cliffs, N.J.: Prentice-Hall, Inc.

Vannier, Maryhelen, and Poindexter, Hally Beth. 1960. *Individual and team sports for girls and women*. Philadelphia: W.B. Saunders Co.

Varner, Margaret. 1966. *Badminton*. Dubuque, Iowa: Wm. C Brown Co.

Weston, Arthur. *The making of American physical education*. New York: Appleton-Century-Crofts.

PERSONALITIES IN BADMINTON

A badminton queen. 1951. *Bird Chatter*, January-February, p. 7.

Gustavson, Leland. 1956. Ken Davidson's early years in America. *Bird Chatter*, January-February, p. 4.

Indonesian wins at badminton. 1959. *Life Magazine*, April 20, pp. 67-68.

Recipients of Helms Awards. 1956. *Bird Chatter*, March-April, pp. 14-15.
The talk of the town. 1954. *The New Yorker*, April 17, p. 24.

SCORING

Official scoresheet and procedure. 1954-56. *Tennis-badminton guide*. DGWS, pp. 99-100.
Scoring. 1950-1952. *Tennis-badminton guide*. DGWS, p. 32.

SKILLS AND STRATEGY

Davidson, Kenneth R., and Gustavson, L. R. 1954. Badminton stroke production. *Scholastic Coach*, February, p. 22.
Forgie, Hugh. 1951. Effective shots. *Bird Chatter*, January-February, p. 9.
——— 1958. Badminton. *Selected tennis-badminton articles*. DGWS, pp. 88-95.
——— 1956. Court tactics. *Bird Chatter*, January-February, p. 8.
Grant, Doug. 1951. Net strokes. *Bird Chatter*, March-April, p. 6.
——— 1952. The forehand drive. *Bird Chatter*, April.
——— 1953. The high backhand. *Bird Chatter*, June.
Gustavson, Leland. 1956. Elementary advice on smashing. *Bird Chatter*, January-February, p. 20.
——— 1956. Elementary grip and stroking. *Bird Chatter*, January-February, p. 5.
Poole, Jim. 1960. The backhand. *Bird Chatter*, November-December, p. 11.
Rutledge, Abbie. 1955. Badminton skills and strategy. *Journal of Health, Physical Education and Recreation*, May, pp. 21-22.
Varner, Margaret. 1963. Ideas for developing skill in badminton. *Bird Chatter*, January-February, p. 12.
——— 1963. Ideas for developing skill in badminton. *Bird Chatter*, March-April, pp. 12-13.

HISTORY

Russell, Bruce. 1950. Badminton evolution. *Bird Chatter*, November-December, pp. 20-21.
Sickles, Richard. 1958. History highlights. *Selected tennis-badminton articles*. DGWS, pp. 71-75.

SELF-INSTRUCTION

Davidson, Kenneth R. 1950. Badminton, footwork, and body balance. *Scholastic Coach*, p. 16.

———— 1958. The importance of badminton's four basic strokes. *Selected tennis-badminton articles*. DGWS, pp. 75-76.

Day, June. 1963. First lessons in badminton. *Journal of Health, Physical Education and Recreation*, March, pp. 28-31.

Pons, Jeanne E. 1950-1952. Tricks of the trade. *Tennis-badminton guide*. DGWS, pp. 18-21.

———— 1958. Common faults in the basic strokes. *Selected tennis-badminton articles*. DGWS, pp. 96-99.

———— 1958. Key phrases. *Selected tennis-badminton articles*. DGWS, pp. 106-108.

Rogers, Winn. 1958. Badminton tips and techniques. *Selected tennis-badminton articles*. DGWS, pp. 111-14.

Rutledge, Abbie. 1955. Let's teach badminton. *Journal of Health, Physical Education and Recreation*, March, pp. 25-26.

———— 1966. Teaching the adult beginner. *Bird Chatter*, November-December, pp. 12-13.

Smith, K. Maurine. 1956-1958. The role of intention-displaying movements of tennis and badminton. *Tennis-badminton guide*. DGWS, p. 90.

Smith, Lenore C. 1958. Teaching badminton in a coeducational setting. *Selected tennis-badminton articles*. DGWS, pp. 109-10.

SELF-TESTING

Fox, Katherine. 1953. Beginning badminton examination. *Research Quarterly*, May, pp. 135-46.

French, F. L., and Statler, E. 1949. Study of skill tests in badminton for college women. *Research Quarterly*, October, pp. 257-72.

Hennis, Gail. 1956. Badminton knowledge test for college women. *Research Quarterly*, October, p. 301.

Lockhart, A., and McPherson, F. A. 1949. Development of a test of badminton playing ability. *Research Quarterly*, December, pp. 402-5.

Miller, Frances A. 1958. A badminton wall volley test. *Selected tennis-badminton articles*. DGWS, pp. 124-27.

TOURNAMENT TIPS

American Badminton Association. *Official handbook*. 20 Wamesit Rd., Waban, Mass.: American Badminton Association.

Bunn, John W. 1957. *The art of officiating sports*, 2nd ed. Englewood Cliffs, N.J.: Prentice-Hall, Inc.

Hill, LeRoy. 1954-1956. How to run a tournament. *Tennis-badminton guide*. DGWS, pp. 78-79.

Richardson, Don. 1955. Malaya retains Thomas Cup. *Bird Chatter*, November-December, p. 5.

Tourneys and topics. 1950. *Bird Chatter*, March-April, pp. 10-16.

United States championship. 1951. *Bird Chatter*, March-April, pp. 4-5.

DISTRIBUTORS OF VISUAL AIDS

All American Productions, P.O. Box 801, Riverside, Calif. 92502.

Athletic Institute, Merchandise Mart, Room 805, Chicago 54, Ill. 60654.

Frank Church Films, 6117 Grove St., Oakland 9, Calif. 94609.

Coronet Instructional Films, 65 E. South Water St., Chicago, Ill. 60601.

James B. Dick, Co., 719 W. Olympic Blvd., Los Angeles, Calif. 90015.

Educational Productions, Inc., 915 Howard St., San Francisco, Calif. 94103.

General Sportcraft Co., Ltd., 215 Fourth Ave., New York, N.Y. 10003.

Magall's Sound Motion Picture Film Library, 68 W. 48th St., New York, N.Y. 10036.

Pictorial Films, Inc., 106 E. 106th St., New York, N.Y. 10025.

Victor Sports, Inc., 4512 Packers Ave., Chicago 9, Ill, 60609.

INDEX